ALL-IN-ONE

PIANO SCALES, CHORDS & ARPEGGIOS

For All Piano Methods

By Karen Harrington

HAL•LEONARD®
7777 W. BLUEMOUND RD. P.O. BOX 13819 MILWAUKEE, WI 53213

ISBN 978-1-4950-8441-6

In Australia Contact:
Hal Leonard Australia Pty. Ltd.
4 Lentara Court
Cheltenham, Victoria, 3192 Australia
Email: ausadmin@halleonard.com.au

Visit Hal Leonard Online at
www.halleonard.com

CONTENTS

INTRODUCTION

Scales

Scales form the basis of Western tonal music, the music to which most of us are accustomed. The chromatic scale is a series of twelve tones separated by semitones (half steps). In Western music, the half step is the smallest interval. A scale may begin on any key and ascend or descend to the next key of the same name.

The *major scale* uses a pattern of whole steps and half steps and may begin on any key. Using W for whole step and H for half step, the pattern for a major scale is as follows:

Major Scale

The pattern for the minor scale varies, depending on the form. The forms are natural minor (pure), which uses the same notes as those of its relative major key; harmonic minor, which is played with the seventh tone raised one half step; and melodic minor, which is played with sixth and seventh tones both raised one half step when ascending and lowered or played in the natural form when descending.

Tetrachords on the Keyboard

The word *tetra* means four. A *tetrachord* is a series of four notes that has a pattern of whole step, whole step, half step. A major scale is made up of two tetrachords separated by a whole step.

On this diagram: W = whole step   H = half step

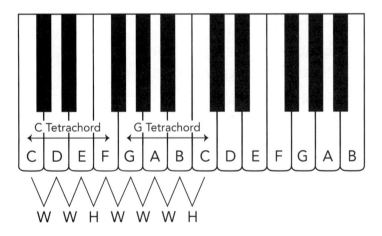

Scale Degrees

The seven notes of major and minor scales have specific numbers, Roman numerals, and names, called *scale degrees*.

The primary (most important) degrees of the scale are:

Tonic: first degree of the scale

Subdominant: fourth degree of the scale

Dominant: fifth degree of the scale

Number	Roman numeral	Scale Degree
1.	**I**	**tonic**
2.	II	supertonic
3.	III	mediant
4.	**IV**	**subdominant**
5.	**V**	**dominant**
6.	VI	submediant
7.	VII	leading tone

Scale Fingerings

Fingerings for most scales fall into three groups.

Group I

C, G, D, A, E major and minor
Note: Finger #4 falls next to the tonic and is used only once per octave.

RH   1 2 3 1 2 3 4 5

LH   5 4 3 2 1 3 2 1

Group II

B, F♯, C♯ (C♭, G♭, D♭) majors and **B** minor

RH and LH   fingers 2 and 3 play on the two black keys
fingers 2, 3, and 4 play on the three black keys

(B major, LH begins with finger #4)

Group III

F, B♭, E♭, A♭ majors and **F** minor

RH   finger #4 plays B♭

LH   finger #4 plays the fourth degree

Note: F major and minor LH uses the fingering for Group I.

For black key minor scale fingerings, see the correlated scale pages in this book.

Key Signatures

In a scale, the number of sharps and flats denotes the *key signature*. When starting a scale on the second tetrachord, or fifth tone of the scale, a new sharp is added. When moving down a fifth on the keyboard to start a new scale, a flat is added. This is best shown in the *Circle of Fifths*.

Circle of Fifths

The diagram below shows the *Circle of Fifths*. The sharp keys move clockwise by fifths and the flat keys move counter-clockwise by fourths.

There are fifteen major keys. There are seven keys that use sharps, seven keys that use flats, and one key – the key of C – that has no sharps or flats.

There are fifteen minor keys. Each minor key relates to a major key. Each minor key begins on the sixth tone of its related major scale and has the same number of sharps or flats.

At the bottom of the circle are **enharmonic** keys. These keys are the same on the keyboard, but are spelled differently, like F♯ and G♭.

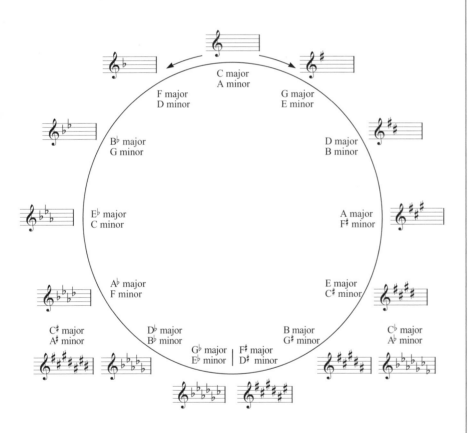

Order of sharps   F C G D A E B

Order of flats   B E A D G C F

(Notice how the order of sharps and flats
are mirror images of each other!)

Chords

Three or more pitches (notes) sounded simultaneously make up a chord. Chords of the scale are built in thirds above each scale degree. A three-note chord is called a *triad*. The *primary chords* are the I, IV, and V. Dominant 7th and diminished 7th chords are also included in this book, as are inversions and cadences.

Arpeggios

An arpeggio is a chord whose notes are played separately. It comes from the word "arpa," meaning harp. This book includes arpeggios for every major and minor scale.

A Note about the layout of the Scales, Chords and Arpeggios in Part Two and Part Three of this book:

Major Scales

Each major scale includes:
- the scale in one, two, three, and four octaves
- the scale in contrary motion
- triads built on each scale degree
- blocked and broken tonic inversions
- cadences and their inversions
- the tonic arpeggio in four octaves

Minor Scales

Each minor scale includes:
- the natural minor scale for two octaves
- the harmonic minor scale in two, three, and four octaves
- the melodic minor scale in two octaves
- triads built on each key of the harmonic minor scale
- blocked and broken tonic inversions
- cadences and inversions for the harmonic form
- tonic arpeggios for four octaves
- diminished arpeggios for two octaves and their inversions

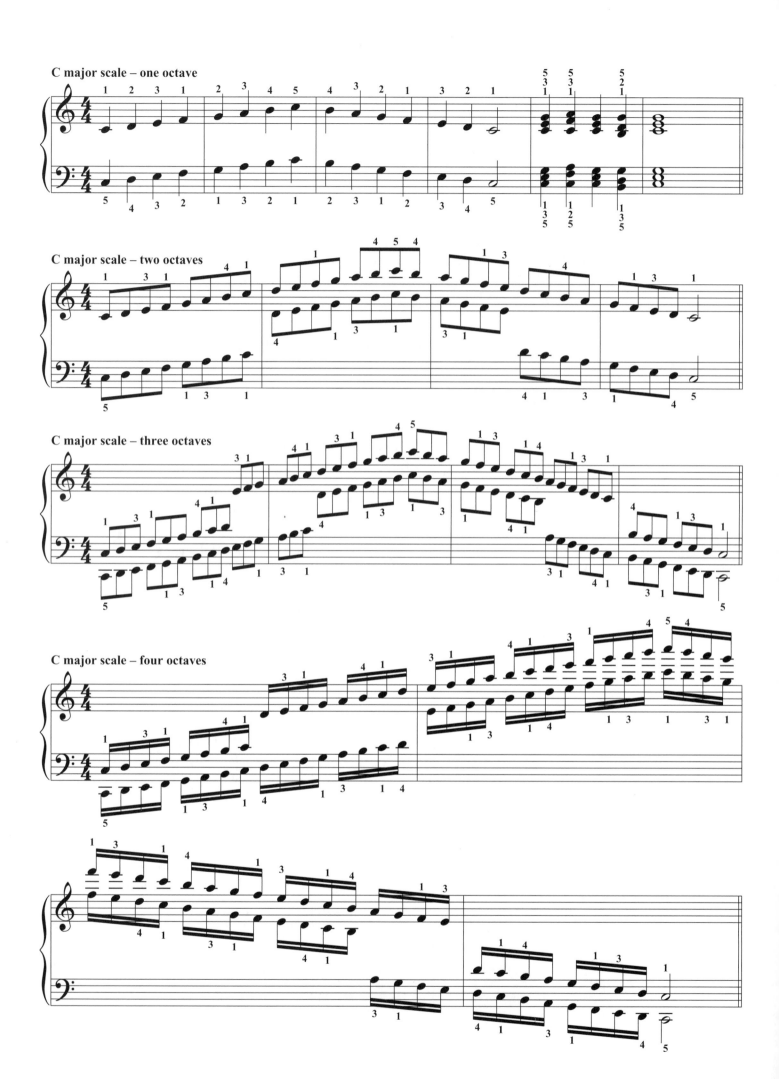

C major scale – two octaves, contrary motion

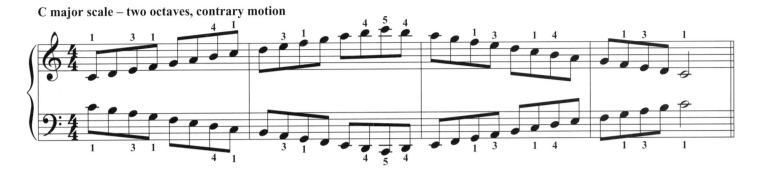

Chords of the scale

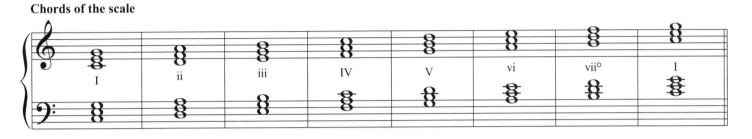

I ii iii IV V vi vii° I

Blocked tonic inversions   **Broken tonic inversions**

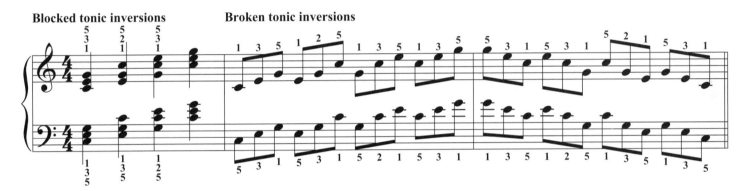

C major cadences – three positions

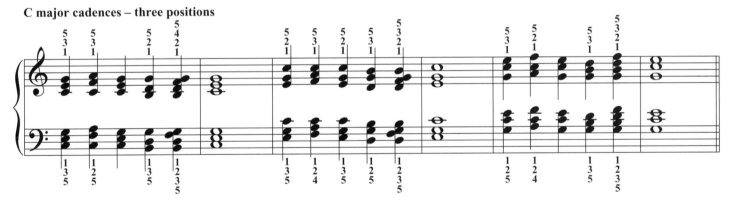

C major arpeggios – four octaves

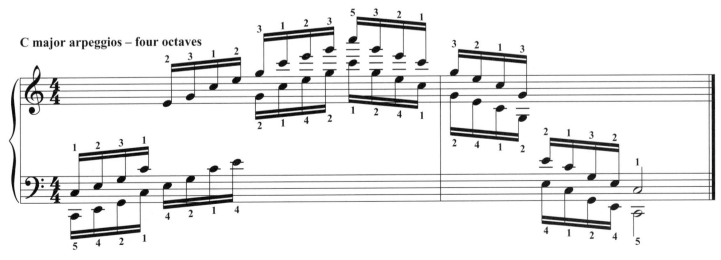

G major scale – one octave

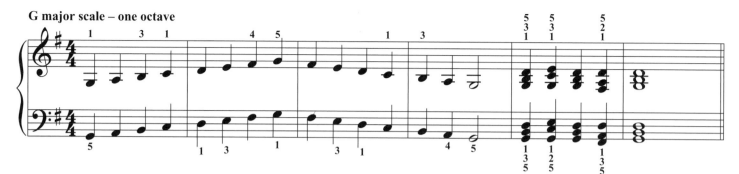

G major scale – two octaves

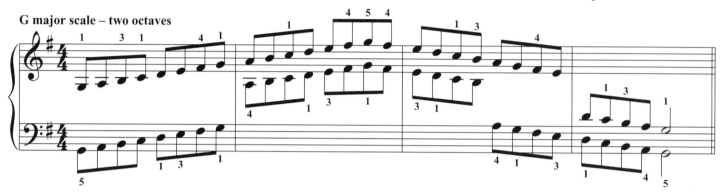

G major scale – three octaves

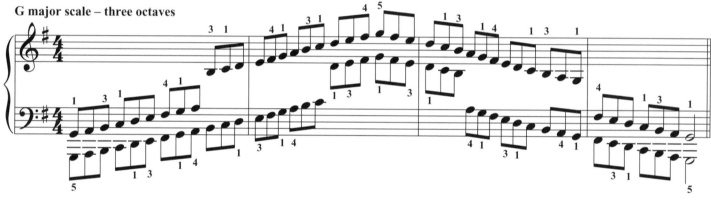

G major scale – four octaves

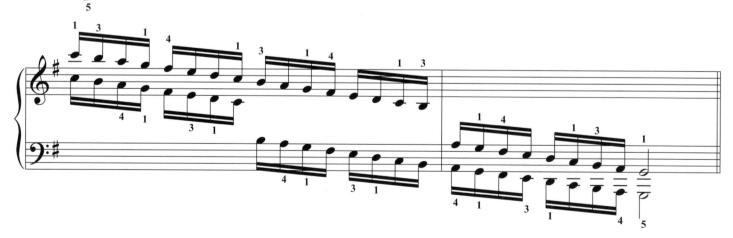

G major scale – two octaves, contrary motion

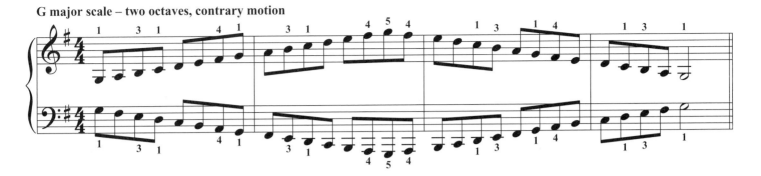

Chords of the scale

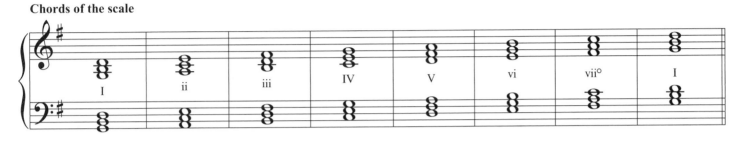

I ii iii IV V vi vii° I

Blocked tonic inversions   **Broken tonic inversions**

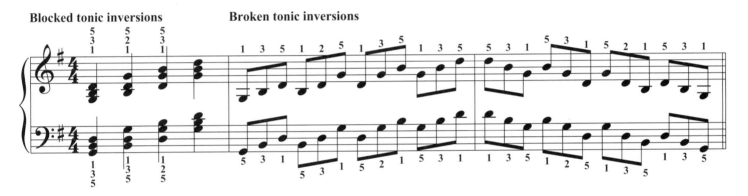

G major cadences – three positions

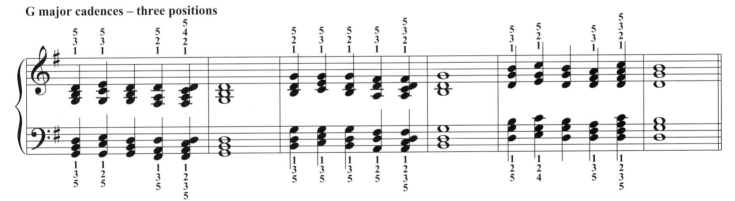

G major arpeggios – four octaves

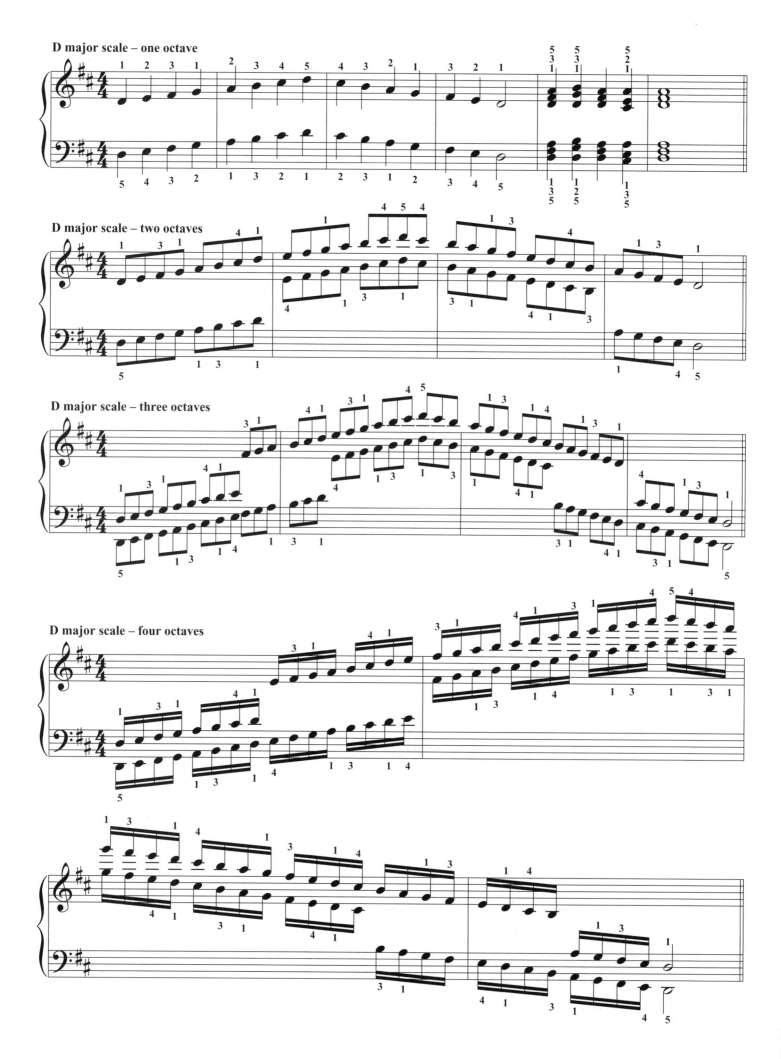

D major scale – one octave

D major scale – two octaves

D major scale – three octaves

D major scale – four octaves

D major scale – two octaves, contrary motion

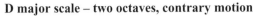

Chords of the scale

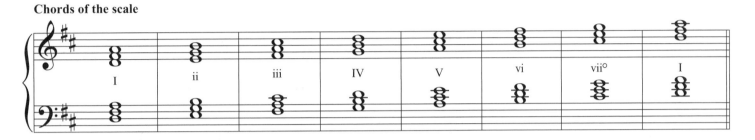

I   ii   iii   IV   V   vi   vii°   I

Blocked tonic inversions   **Broken tonic inversions**

D major cadences – three positions

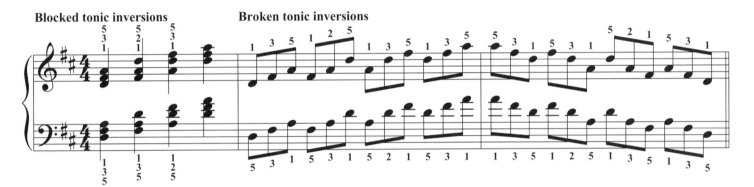

D major arpeggios – four octaves

A major scale – one octave

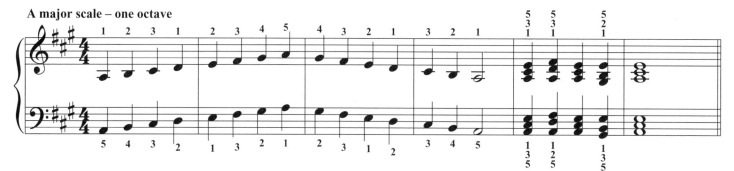

A major scale – two octaves

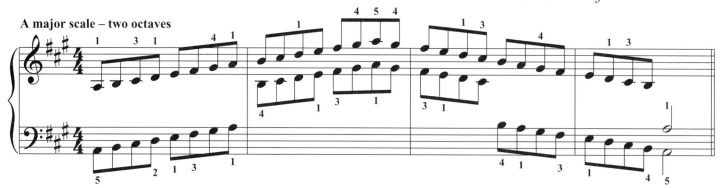

A major scale – three octaves

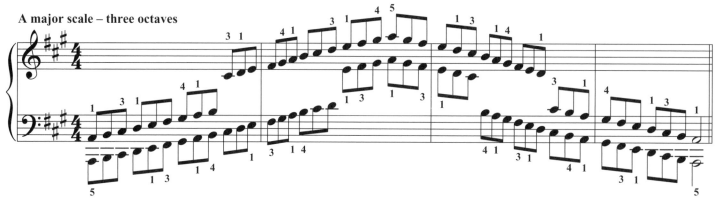

A major scale – four octaves

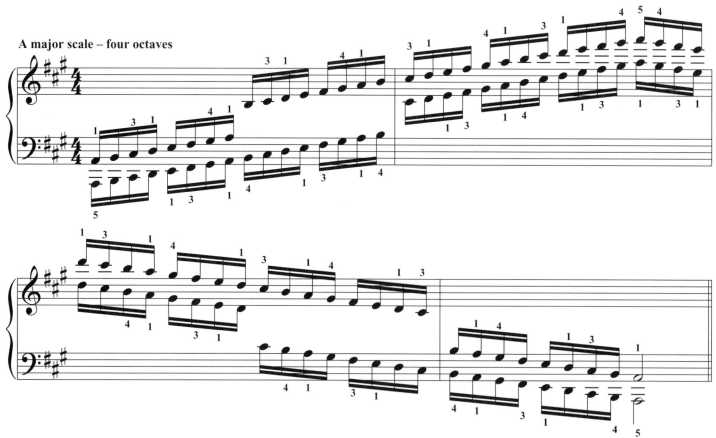

A major scale – two octaves, contrary motion

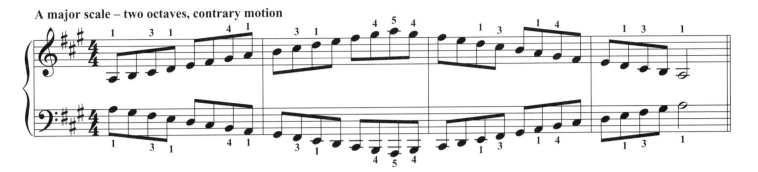

Chords of the scale

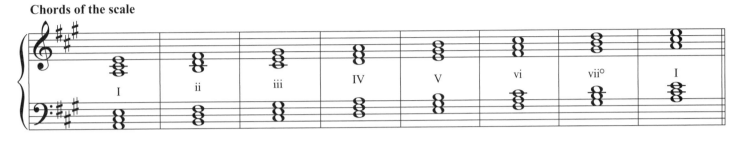

I   ii   iii   IV   V   vi   vii°   I

Blocked tonic inversions   **Broken tonic inversions**

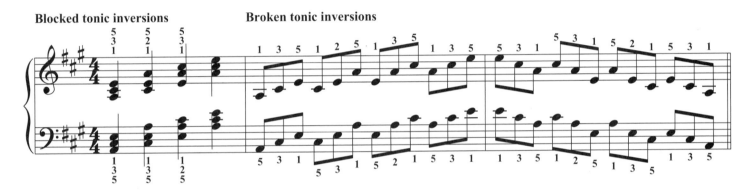

A major cadences – three positions

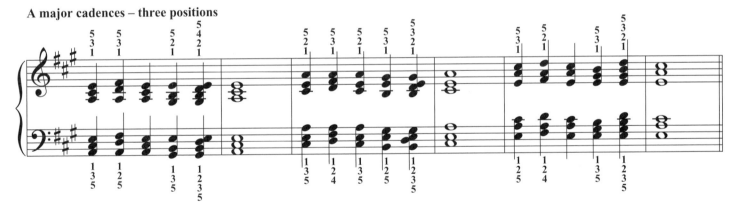

A major arpeggios – four octaves

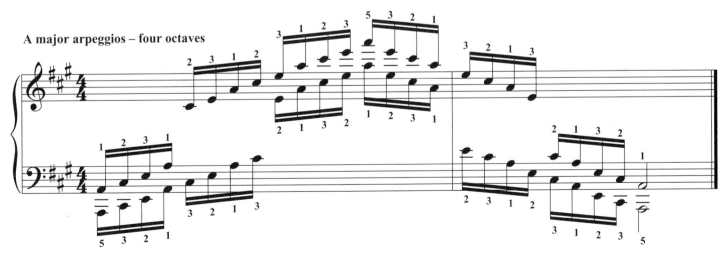

E major scale – one octave

E major scale – two octaves

E major scale – three octaves

E major scale – four octaves

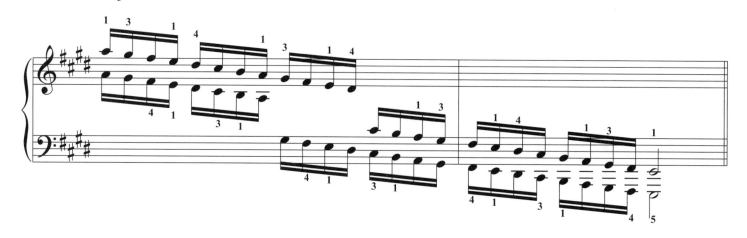

E major scale – two octaves, contrary motion

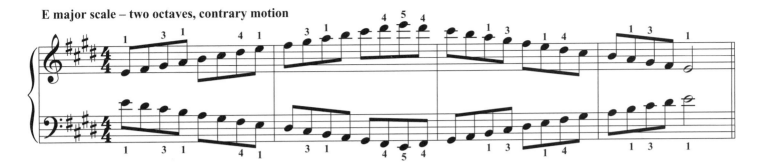

Chords of the scale

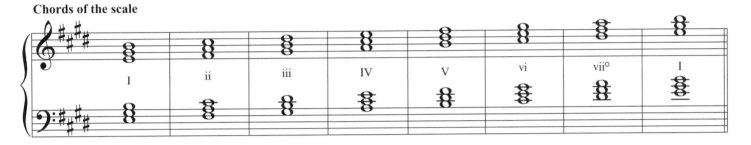

I   ii   iii   IV   V   vi   vii°   I

Blocked tonic inversions   **Broken tonic inversions**

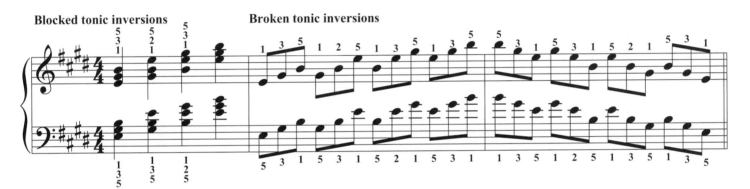

E major cadences – three positions

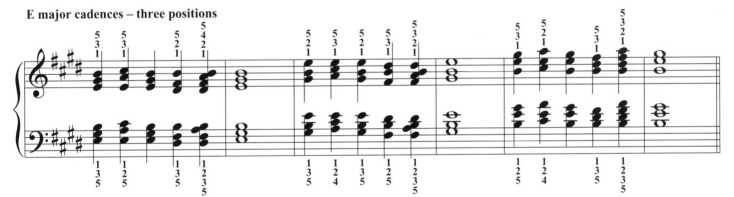

E major arpeggios – four octaves

B major scale – one octave

B major scale – two octaves

B major scale – three octaves

B major scale – four octaves

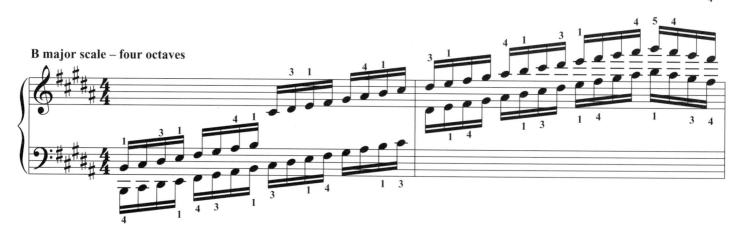

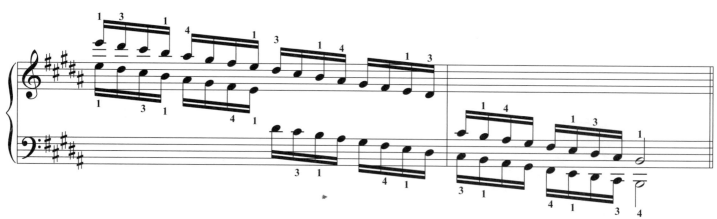

B major scale – two octaves, contrary motion

Chords of the scale

I ii iii IV V vi vii° I

Blocked tonic inversions   **Broken tonic inversions**

B major cadences – three positions

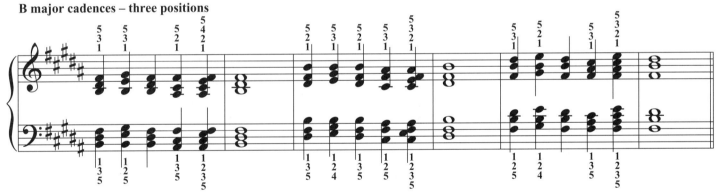

B major arpeggios – four octaves

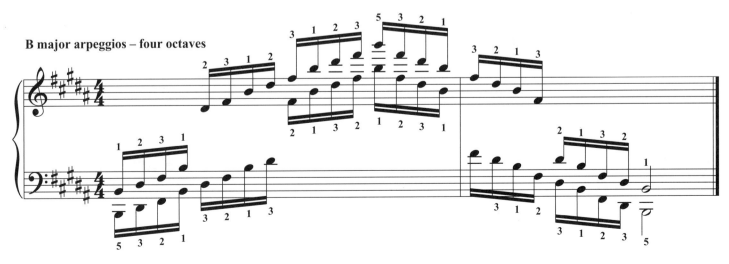

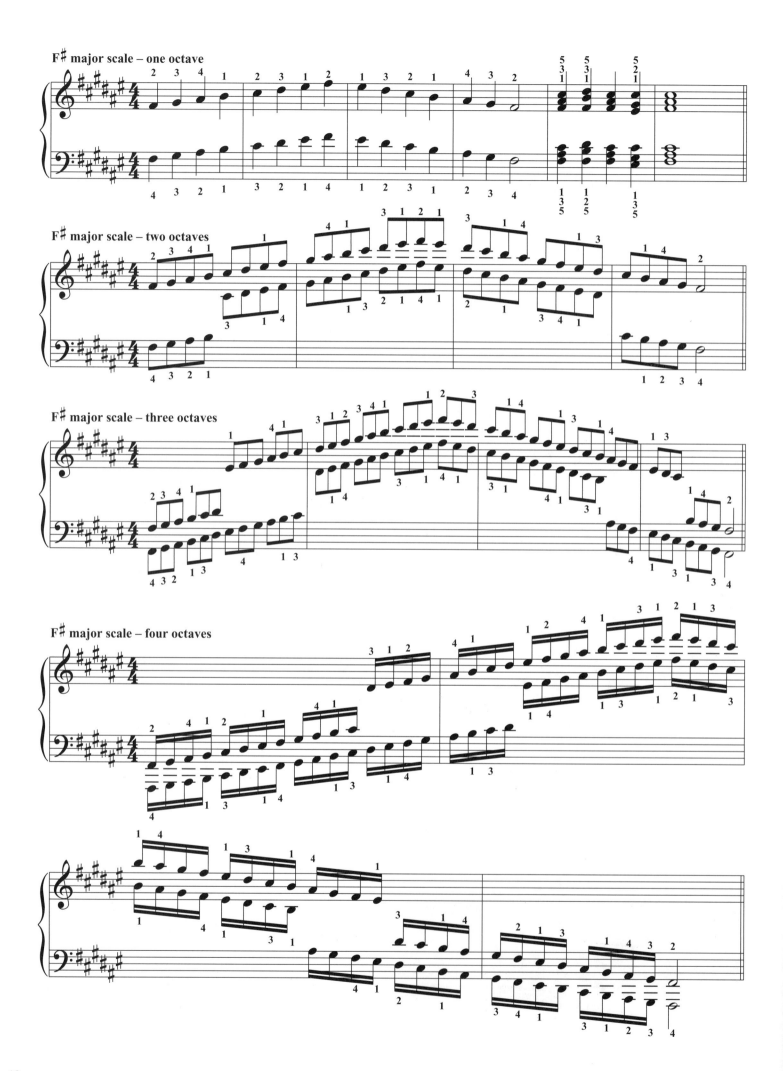

F♯ major scale – two octaves, contrary motion

Chords of the scale

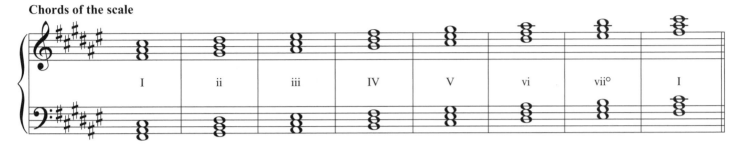

I ii iii IV V vi vii° I

Blocked tonic inversions   **Broken tonic inversions**

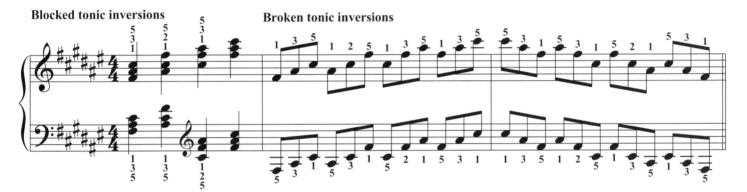

F♯ major cadences – three positions

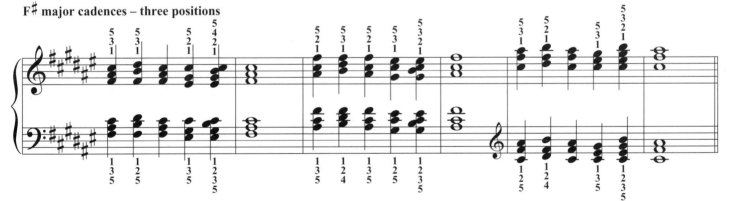

F♯ major arpeggios – four octaves

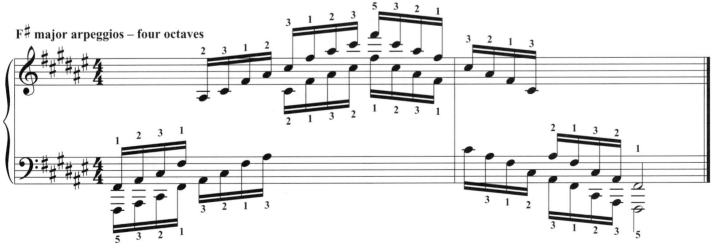

C# major scale – two octaves, contrary motion

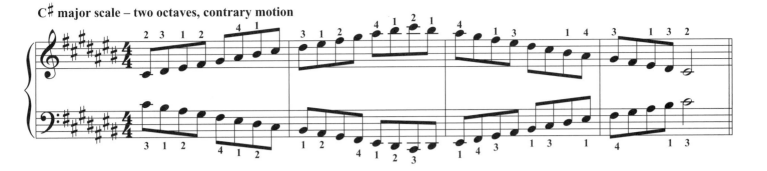

Chords of the scale

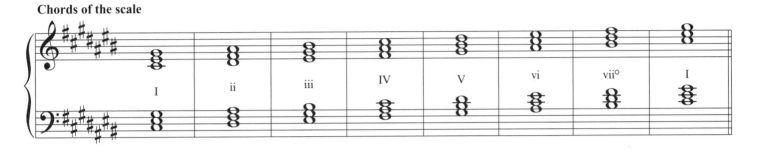

I   ii   iii   IV   V   vi   vii°   I

Blocked tonic inversions   **Broken tonic inversions**

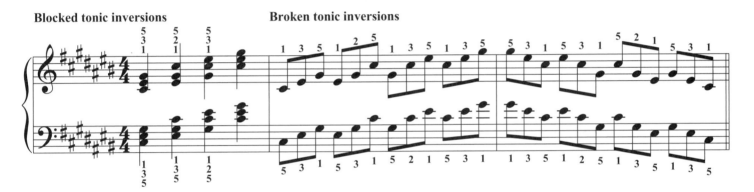

C# major cadences – three positions

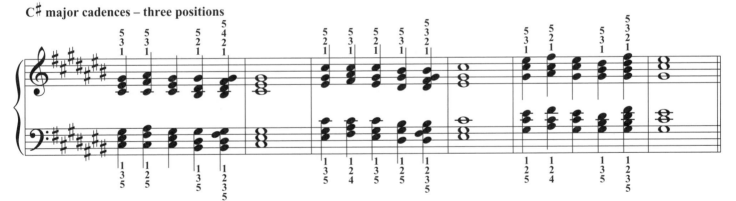

C# major arpeggios – four octaves

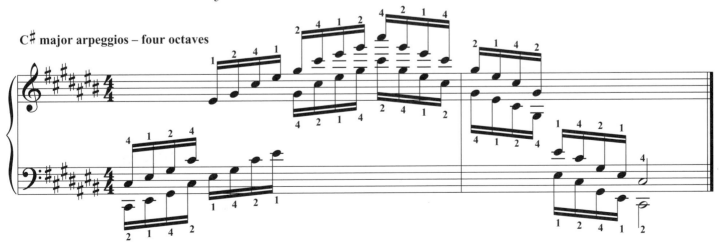

F major scale – one octave

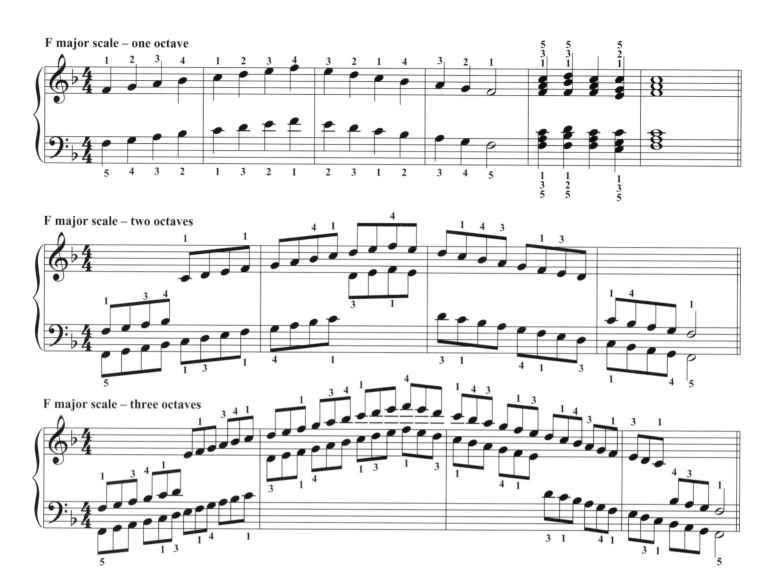

F major scale – two octaves

F major scale – three octaves

F major scale – four octaves

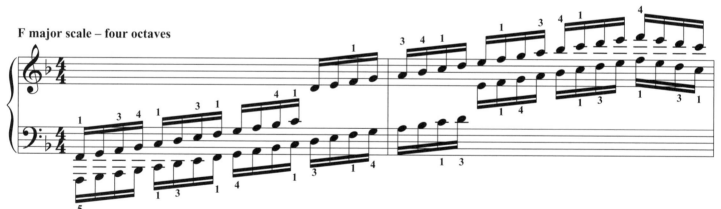

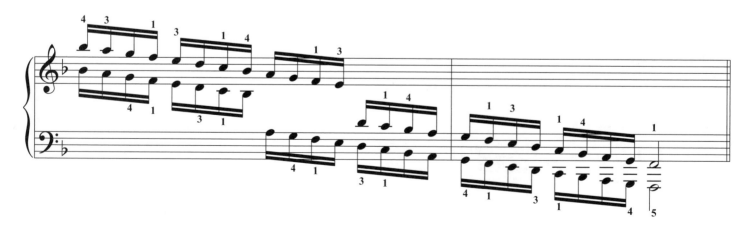

F major scale – two octaves, contrary motion

Chords of the scale

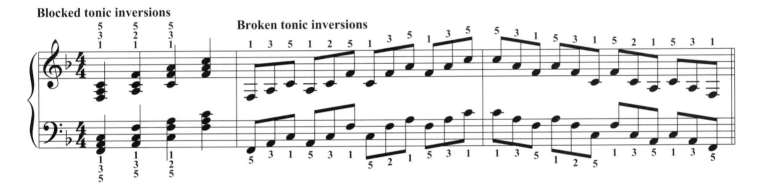

I ii iii IV V vi vii° I

Blocked tonic inversions **Broken tonic inversions**

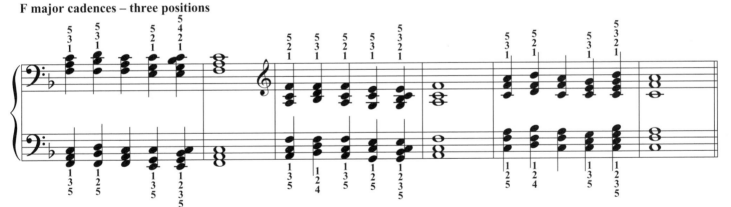

F major cadences – three positions

F major arpeggios – four octaves

23

B♭ major scale – two octaves, contrary motion

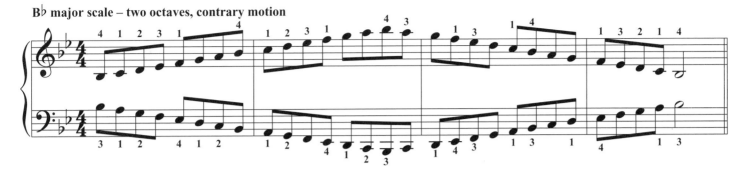

Chords of the scale

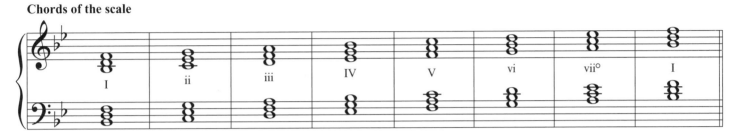

I   ii   iii   IV   V   vi   vii°   I

Blocked tonic inversions   **Broken tonic inversions**

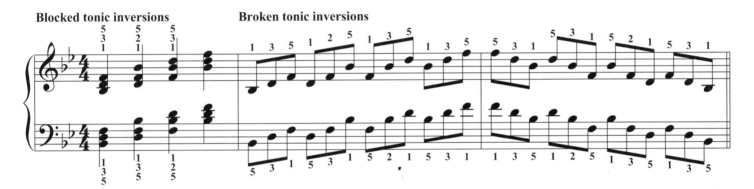

B♭ major cadences – three positions

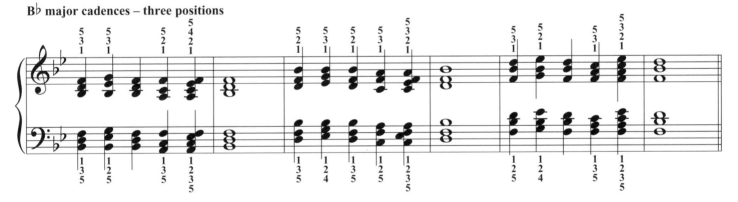

B♭ major arpeggios – four octaves

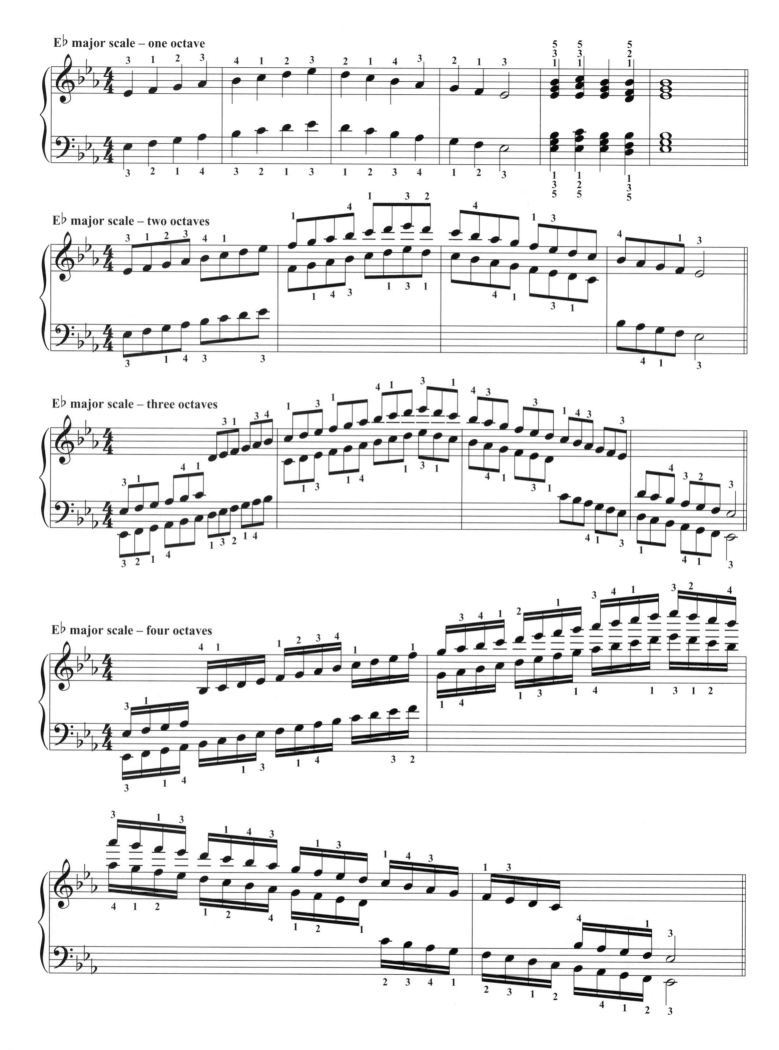

E♭ major scale – two octaves, contrary motion

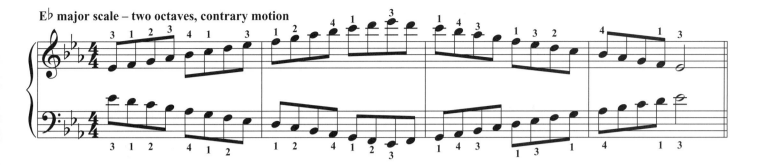

Chords of the scale

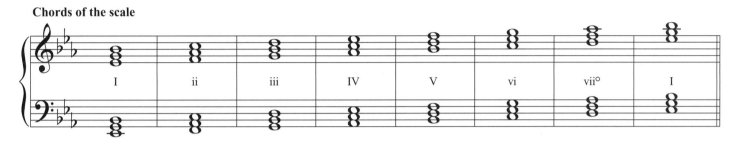

I ii iii IV V vi vii° I

Blocked tonic inversions **Broken tonic inversions**

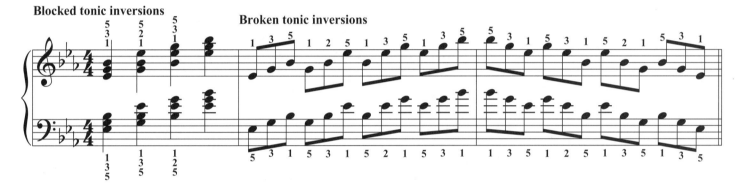

E♭ major cadences – three positions

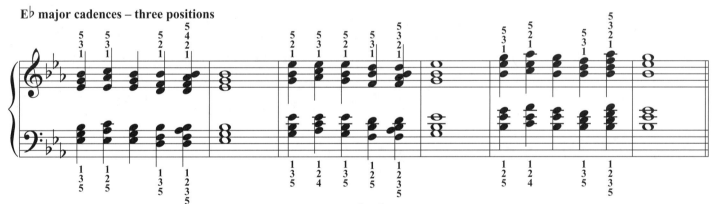

E♭ major arpeggios – four octaves

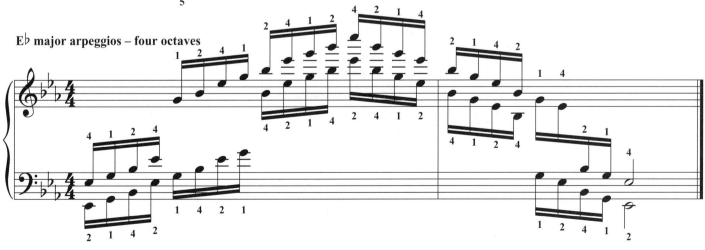

A♭ major scale – two octaves, contrary motion

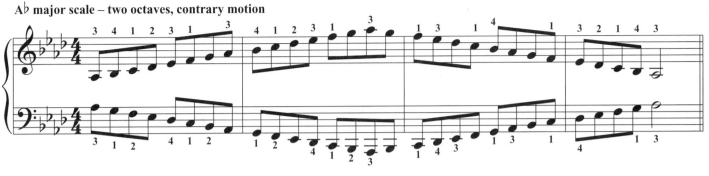

Chords of the scale

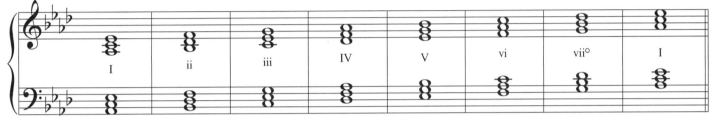

I   ii   iii   IV   V   vi   vii°   I

Blocked tonic inversions   **Broken tonic inversions**

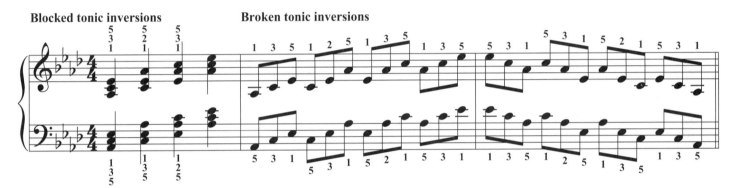

A♭ major cadences – three positions

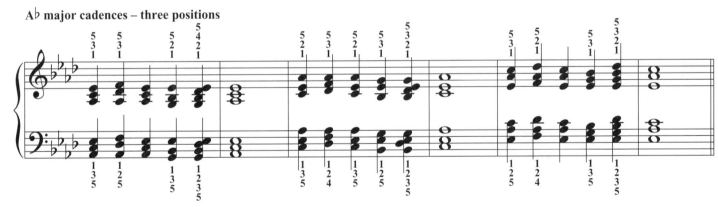

A♭ major arpeggios – four octaves

29

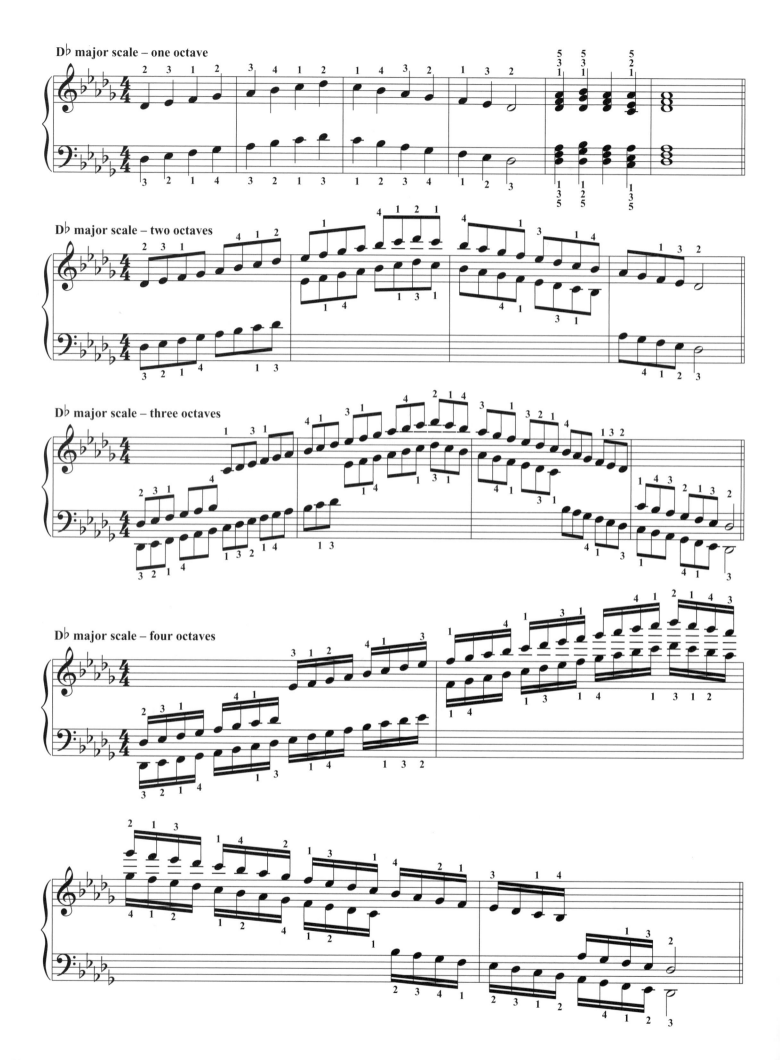

Dь major scale – two octaves, contrary motion

Chords of the scale

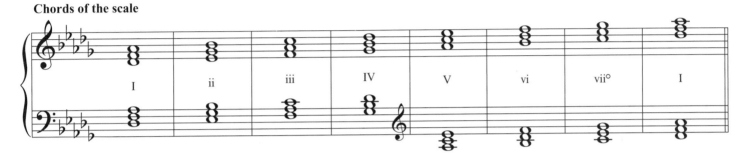

I   ii   iii   IV   V   vi   vii°   I

Blocked tonic inversions   **Broken tonic inversions**

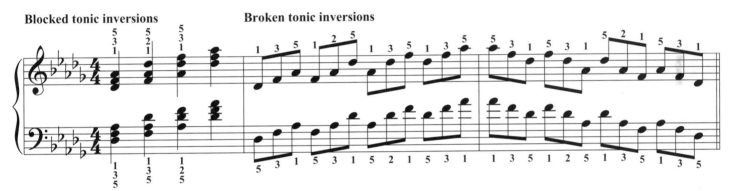

Dь major cadences – three positions

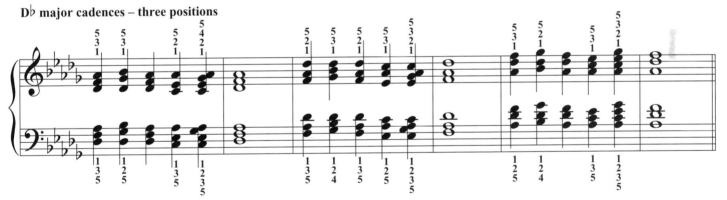

Dь major arpeggios – four octaves

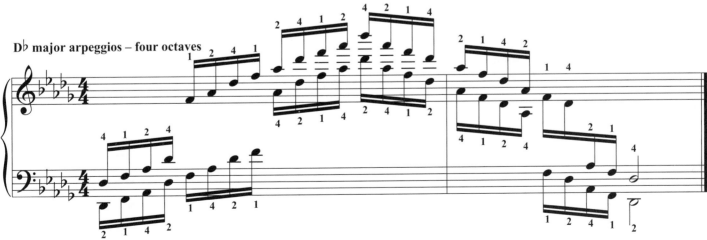

31

G♭ major scale – one octave

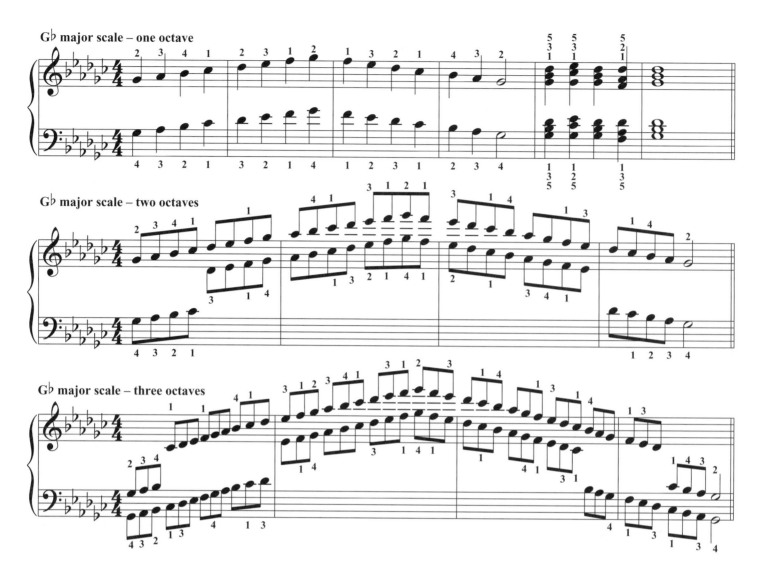

G♭ major scale – two octaves

G♭ major scale – three octaves

G♭ major scale – four octaves

G♭ major scale – two octaves, contrary motion

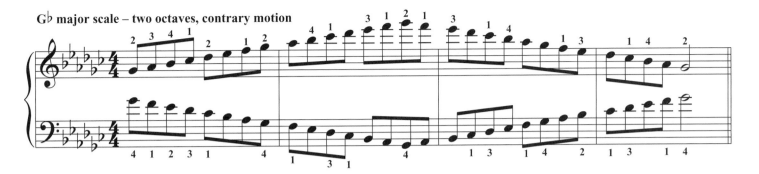

Chords of the scale

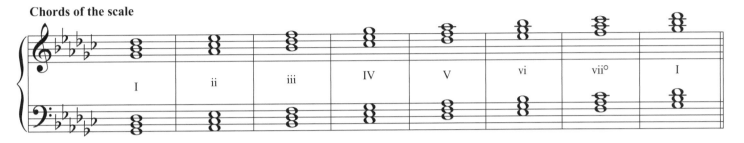

I ii iii IV V vi vii° I

Blocked tonic inversions

Broken tonic inversions

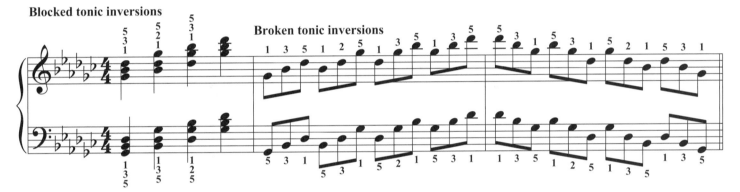

G♭ major cadences – three positions

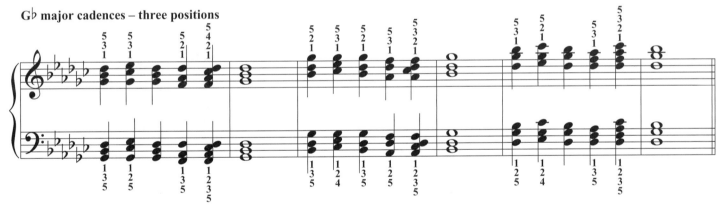

G♭ major arpeggios – four octaves

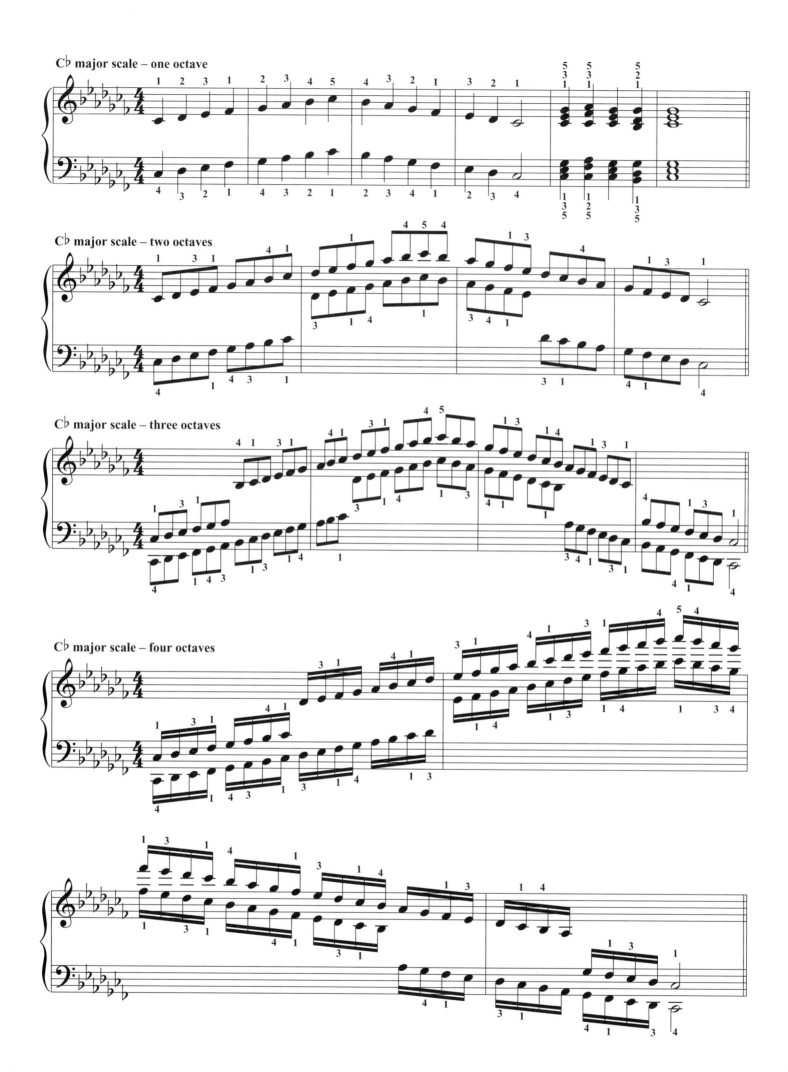

Cb major scale – one octave

Cb major scale – two octaves

Cb major scale – three octaves

Cb major scale – four octaves

C♭ major scale – two octaves, contrary motion

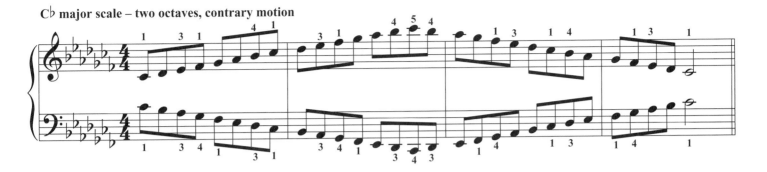

Chords of the scale

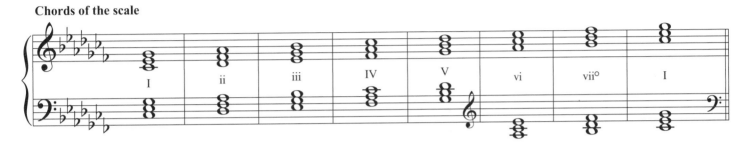

I   ii   iii   IV   V   vi   vii°   I

Blocked tonic inversions   **Broken tonic inversions**

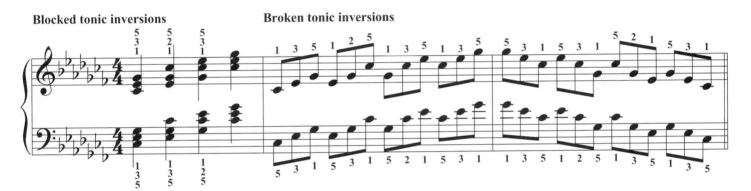

C♭ major cadences – three positions

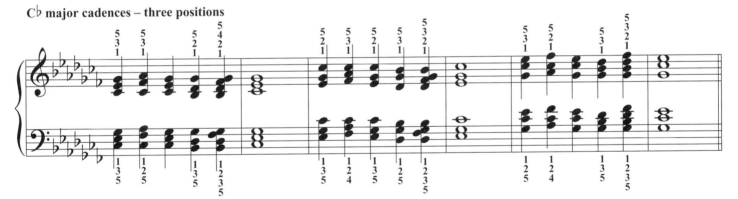

C♭ major arpeggios – four octaves

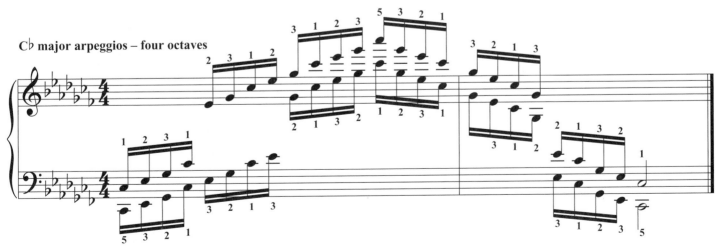

A natural minor scale – two octaves

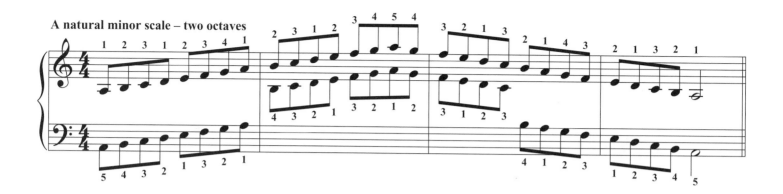

A harmonic minor scale – two octaves

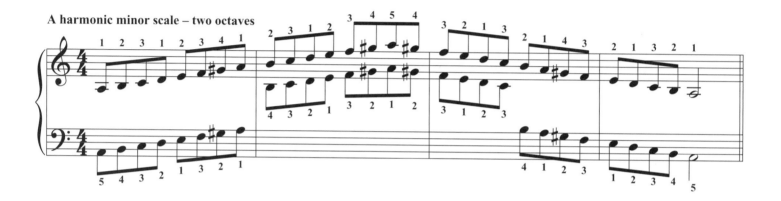

A harmonic minor scale – three octaves

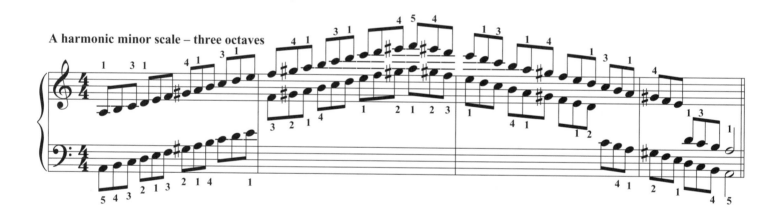

A harmonic minor scale – four octaves

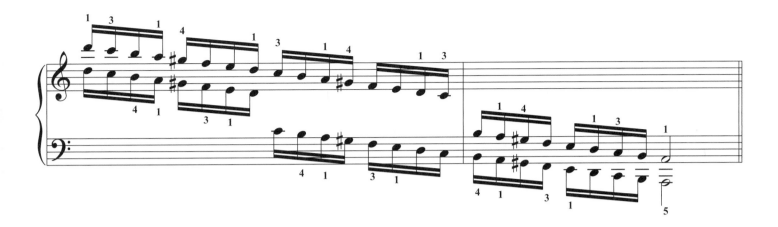

A melodic minor scale – two octaves

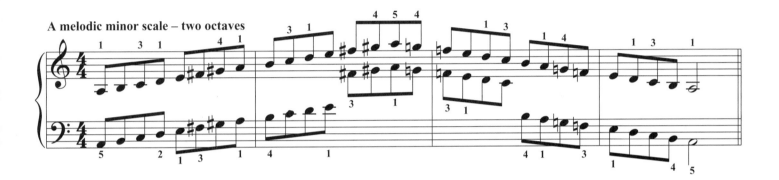

Chords of the A harmonic minor scale

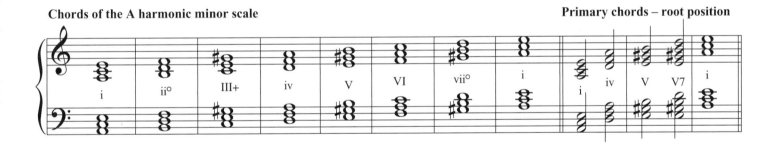

Primary chords – root position

i ii° III+ iv V VI vii° i i iv V V7 i

Blocked tonic inversions

Broken tonic inversions

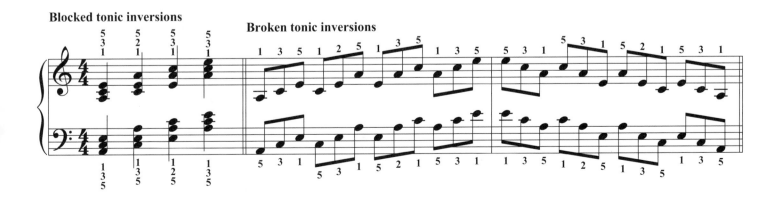

Cadences and inversions

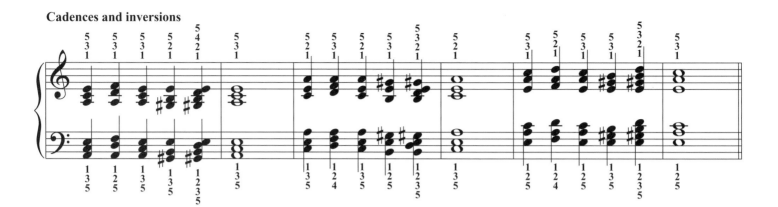

Tonic arpeggios – four octaves

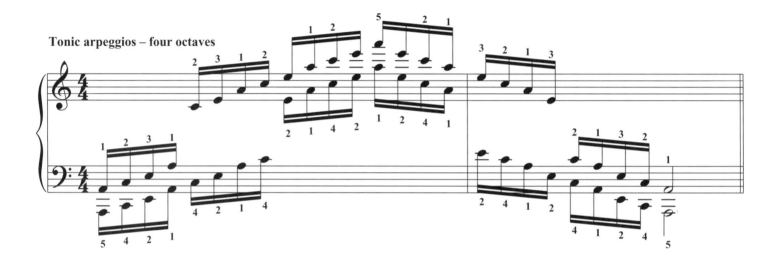

G♯ diminished seventh arpeggios – two octaves, four positions

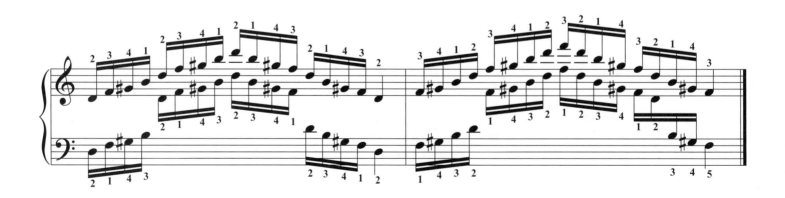

E natural minor scale – two octaves

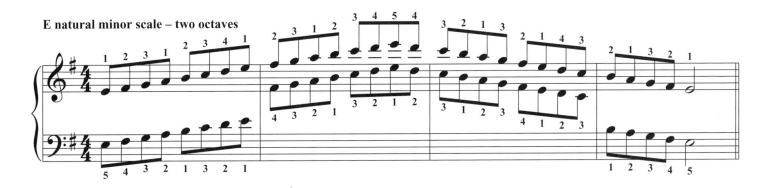

E harmonic minor scale – two octaves

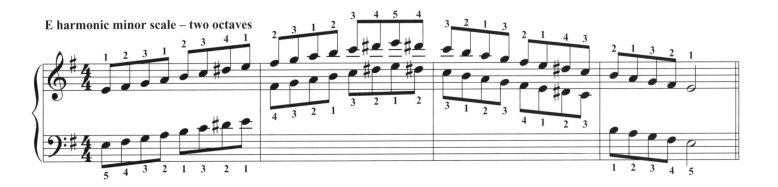

E harmonic minor scale – three octaves

E harmonic minor scale – four octaves

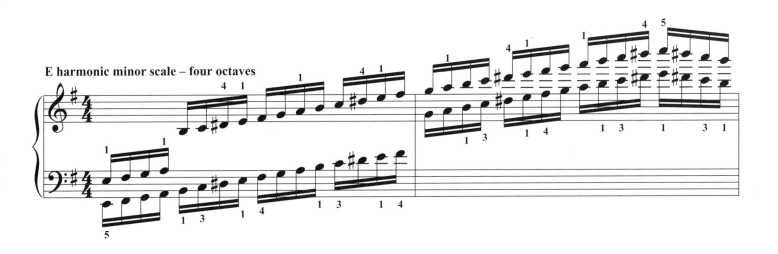

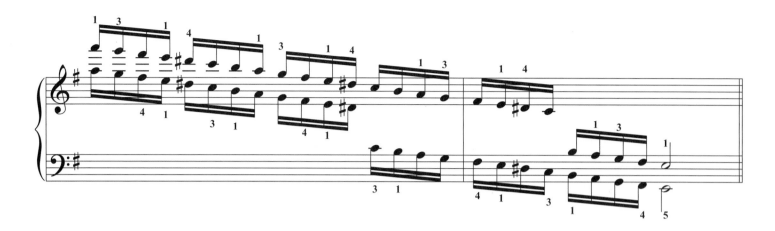

E melodic minor scale – two octaves

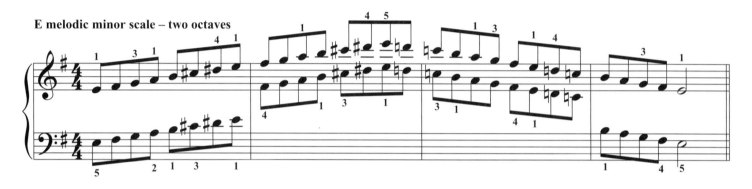

Chords of the E harmonic minor scale

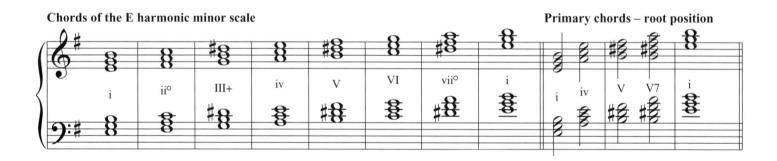

i	ii°	III+	iv	V	VI	vii°	i

Primary chords – root position

i	iv	V	V7	i

Blocked tonic inversions

Broken tonic inversions

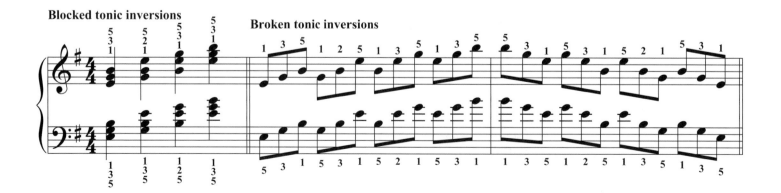

Cadences and inversions

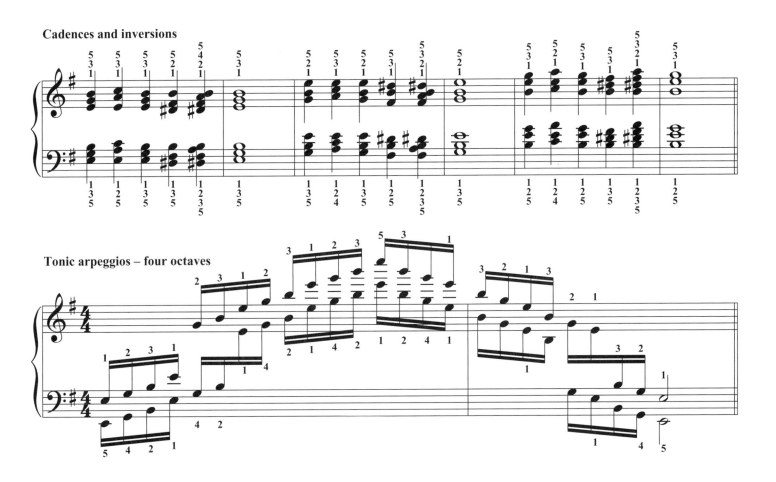

Tonic arpeggios – four octaves

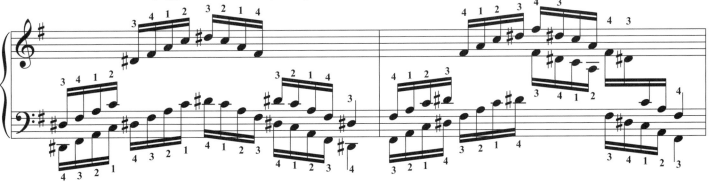

D♯ diminished seventh arpeggios – two octaves, four positions

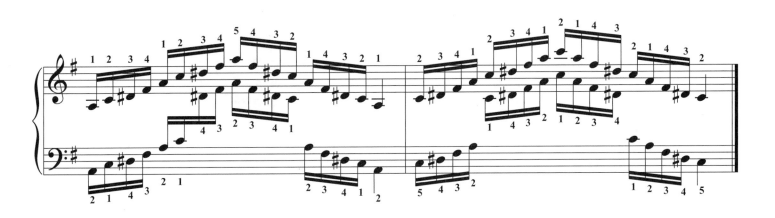

B natural minor scale – two octaves

B harmonic minor scale – two octaves

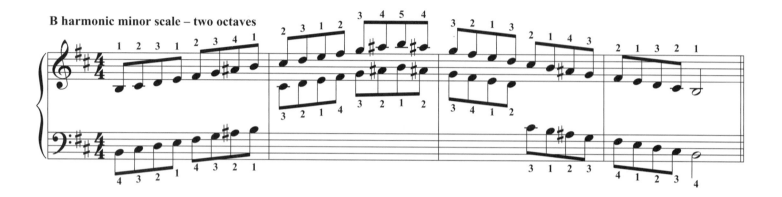

B harmonic minor scale – three octaves

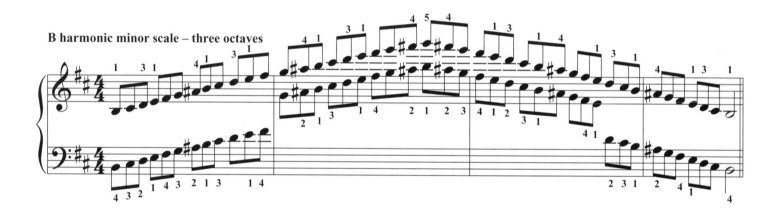

B harmonic minor scale – four octaves

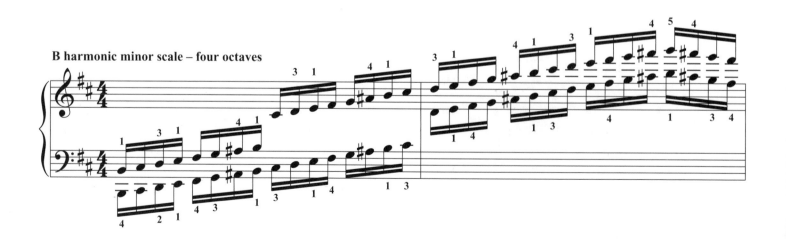

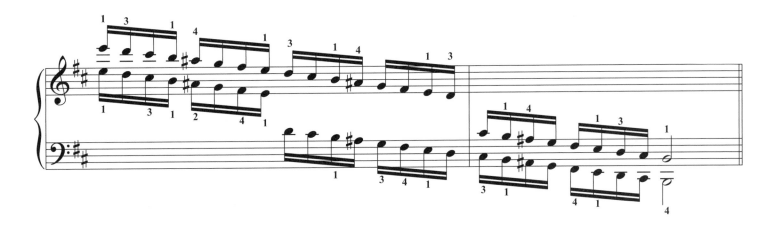

B melodic minor scale – two octaves

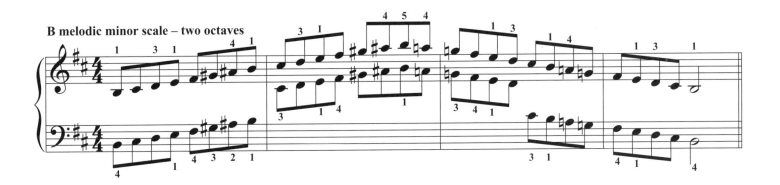

Chords of the B harmonic minor scale

Primary chords – root position

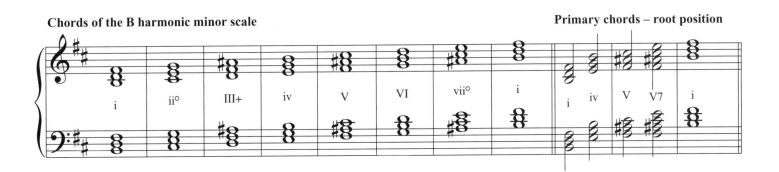

i   ii°   III+   iv   V   VI   vii°   i   i   iv   V   V7   i

Blocked tonic inversions

Broken tonic inversions

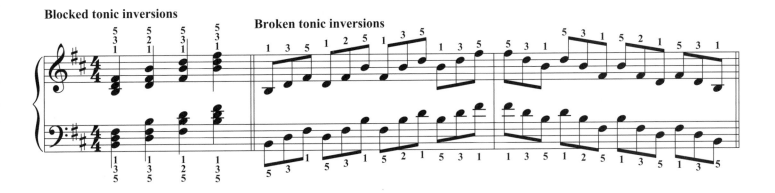

Cadences and inversions

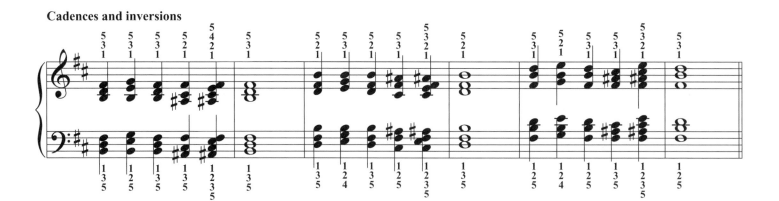

Tonic arpeggios – four octaves

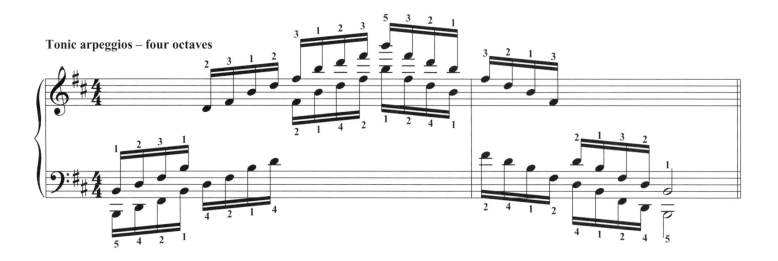

A♯ diminished seventh arpeggios – two octaves, four positions

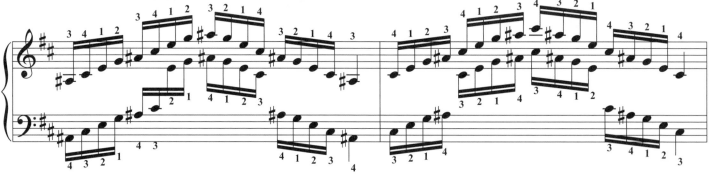

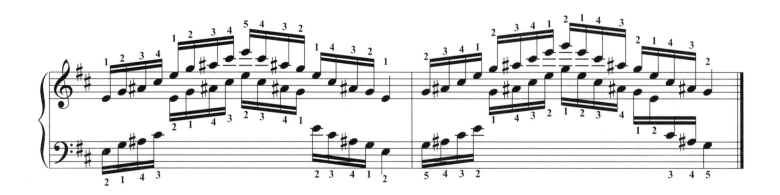

F♯ natural minor scale – two octaves

F♯ harmonic minor scale – two octaves

F♯ harmonic minor scale – three octaves

F♯ harmonic minor scale – four octaves

F♯ melodic minor scale – two octaves

Chords of the F♯ harmonic minor scale

Primary chords – root position

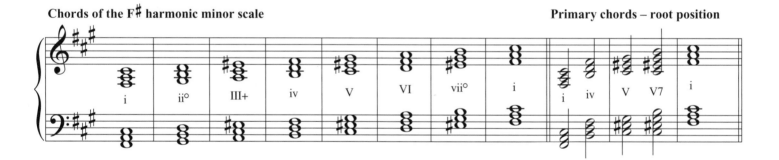

i   ii°   III+   iv   V   VI   vii°   i   i   iv   V   V7   i

Blocked tonic inversions

Broken tonic inversions

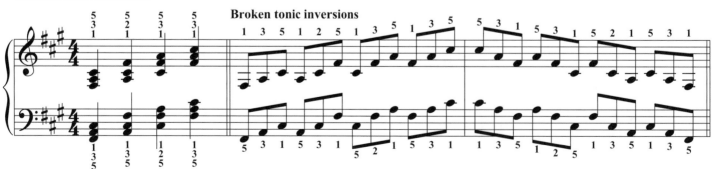

Cadences and inversions

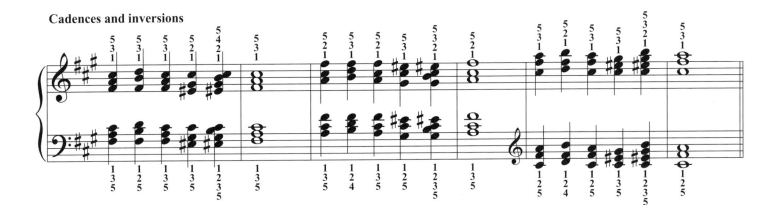

Tonic arpeggios – four octaves

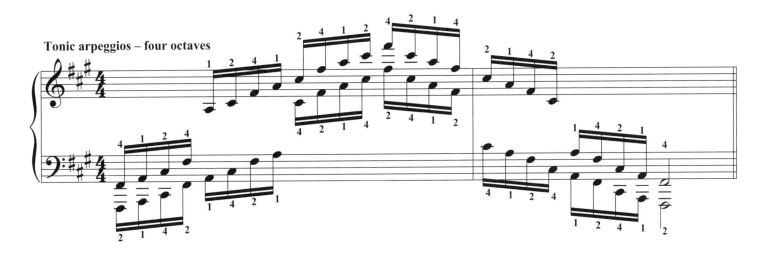

E♯ diminished seventh arpeggios – two octaves, four positions

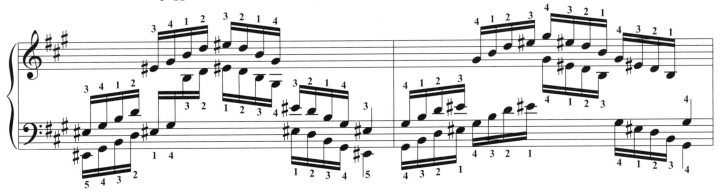

C♯ natural minor scale – two octaves

C♯ harmonic minor scale – two octaves

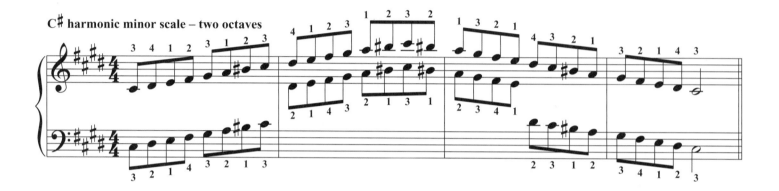

C♯ harmonic minor scale – three octaves

C♯ harmonic minor scale – four octaves

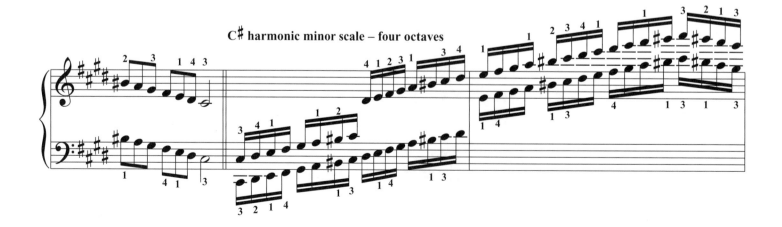

C♯ melodic minor scale – two octaves

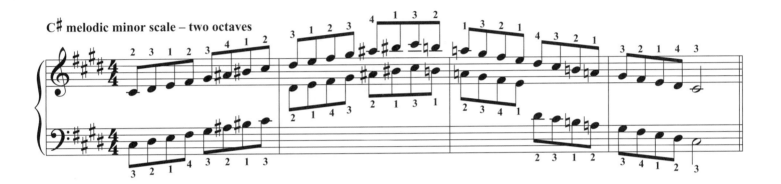

Chords of the C♯ harmonic minor scale

Primary chords – root position

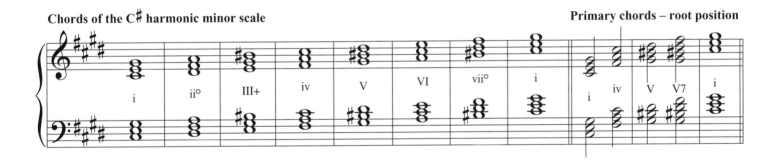

Blocked tonic inversions

Broken tonic inversions

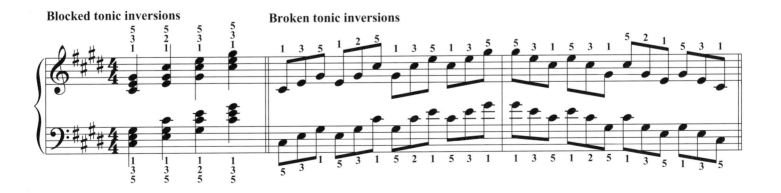

Cadences and inversions

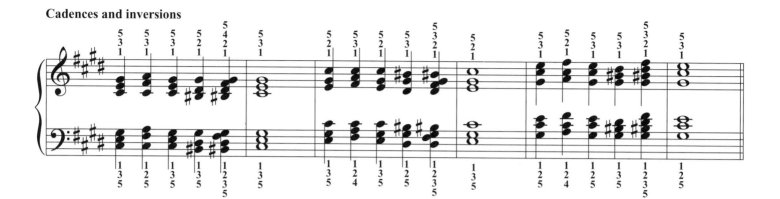

Tonic arpeggios – four octaves

B♯ diminished seventh arpeggios – two octaves, four positions

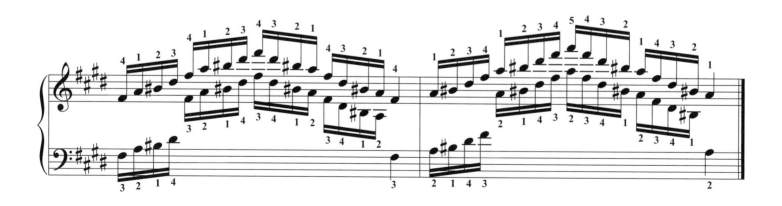

G# natural minor scale – two octaves

G# harmonic minor scale – two octaves

G# harmonic minor scale – three octaves

G# harmonic minor scale – four octaves

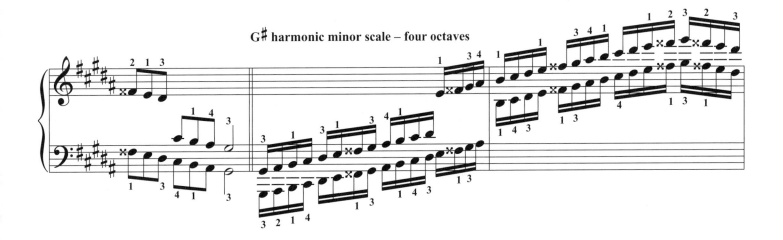

G♯ melodic minor scale – two octaves

Chords of the G♯ harmonic minor scale

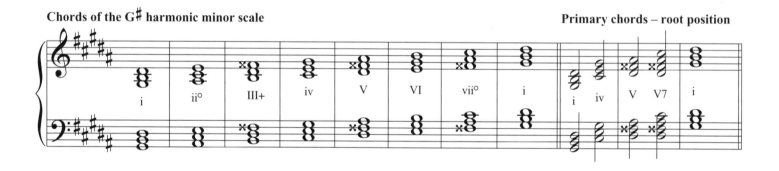

Primary chords – root position

i ii° III+ iv V VI vii° i   i iv V V7 i

Blocked tonic inversions

Broken tonic inversions

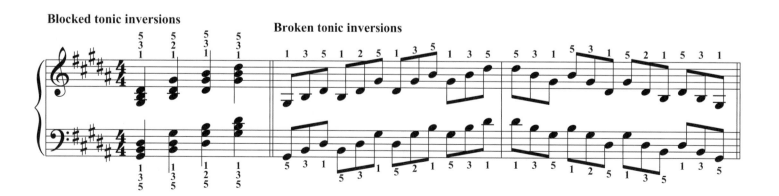

52

Cadences and inversions

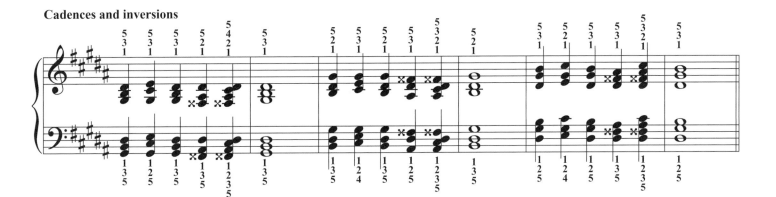

Tonic arpeggios – four octaves

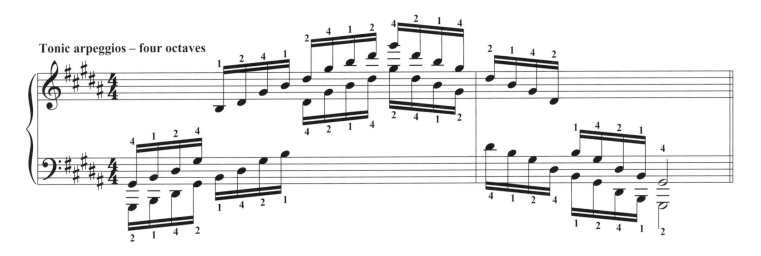

F× diminished seventh arpeggios – two octaves, four positions

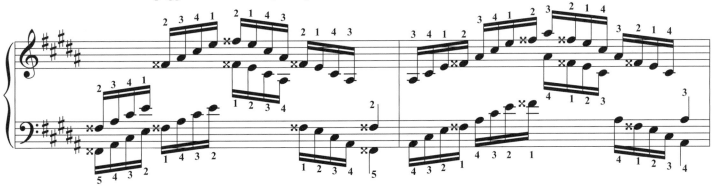

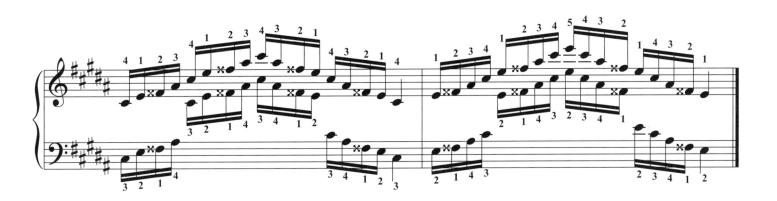

D♯ natural minor scale – two octaves

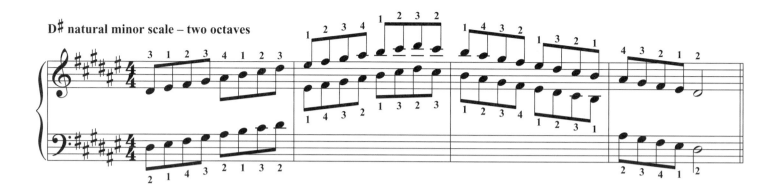

D♯ harmonic minor scale – two octaves

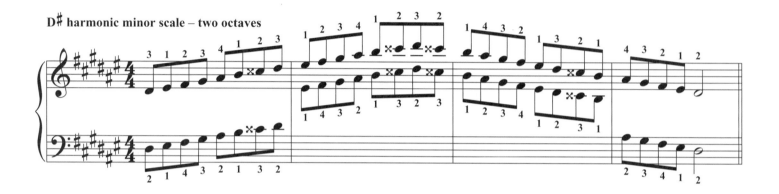

D♯ harmonic minor scale – three octaves

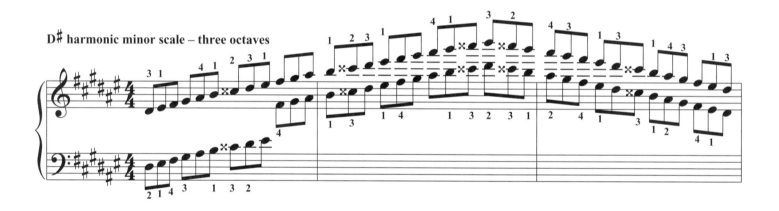

D♯ harmonic minor scale – four octaves

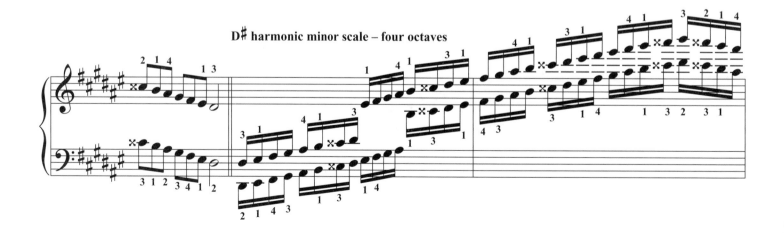

D♯ melodic minor scale – two octaves

Chords of the D♯ harmonic minor scale

Primary chords – root position

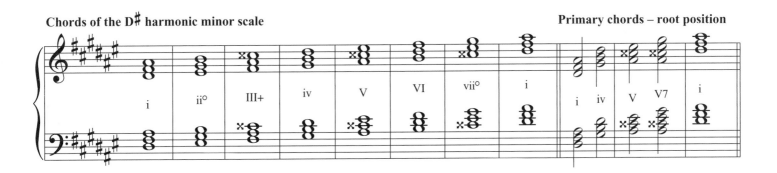

i   ii°   III+   iv   V   VI   vii°   i

i   iv   V   V7   i

Blocked tonic inversions

Broken tonic inversions

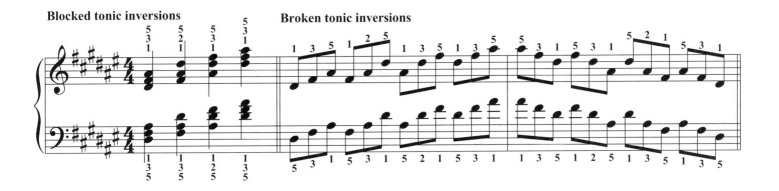

Cadences and inversions

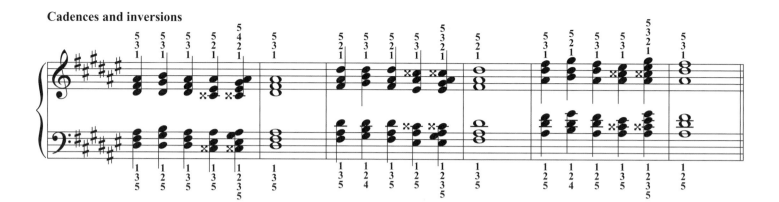

Tonic arpeggios — four octaves

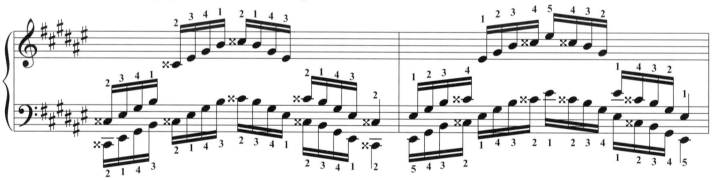

C× diminished seventh arpeggios – two octaves, four positions

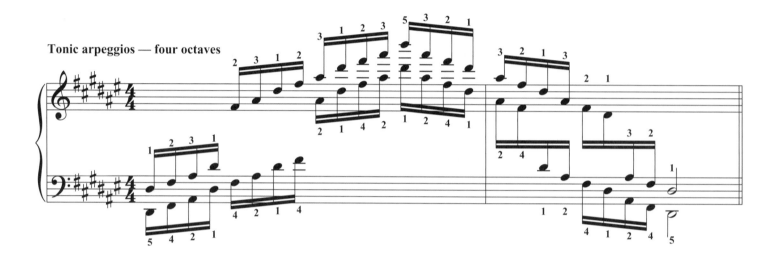

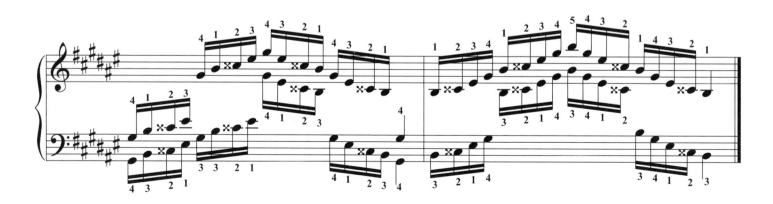

A# natural minor scale – two octaves

A# harmonic minor scale – two octaves

A# harmonic minor scale – three octaves

A# harmonic minor scale – four octaves

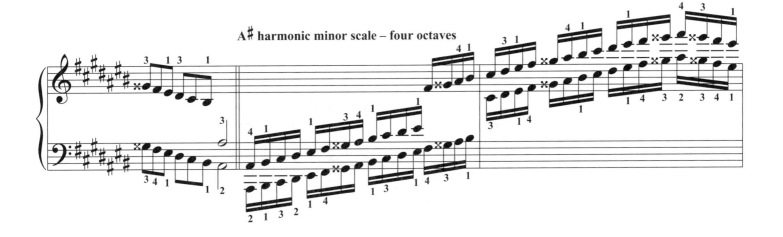

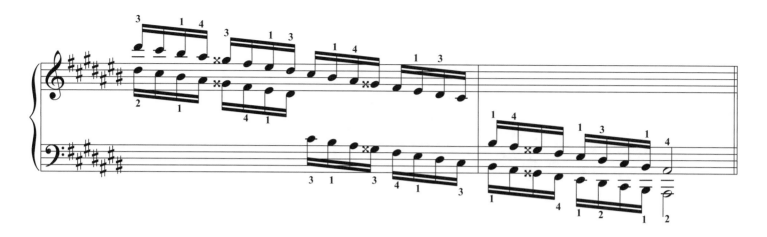

A♯ melodic minor scale – two octaves

Chords of the A♯ harmonic minor scale

Primary chords – root position

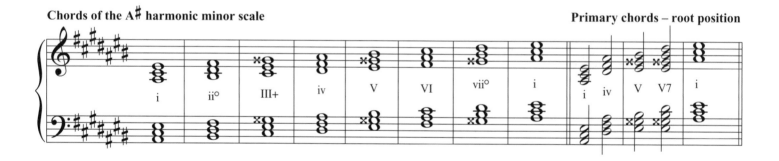

i   ii°   III+   iv   V   VI   vii°   i   i   iv   V   V7   i

Blocked tonic inversions   **Broken tonic inversions**

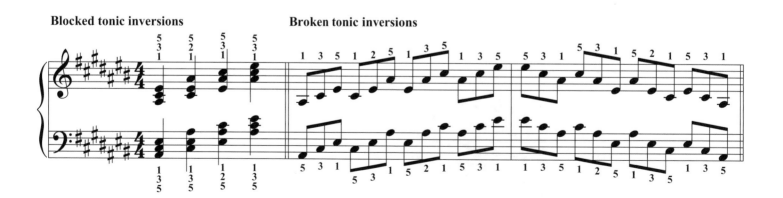

Cadences and inversions

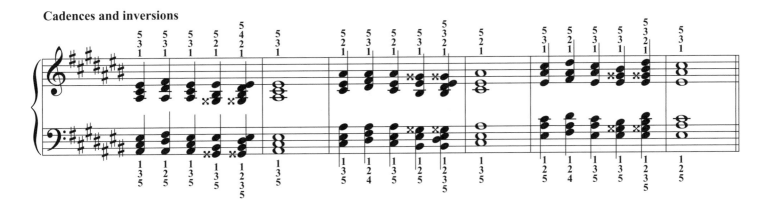

Tonic arpeggios – four octaves

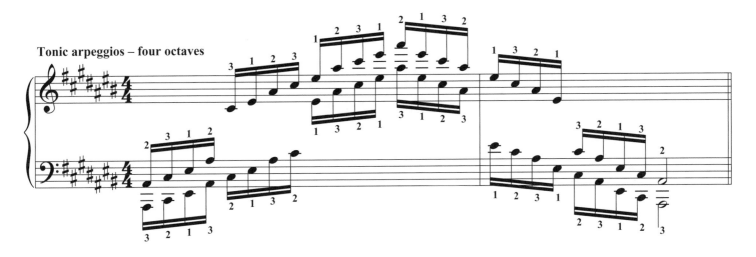

G✕ diminished seventh arpeggios – two octaves, four positions

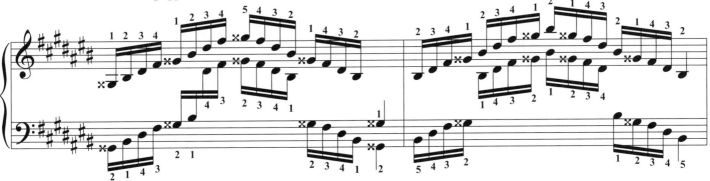

D natural minor scale – two octaves

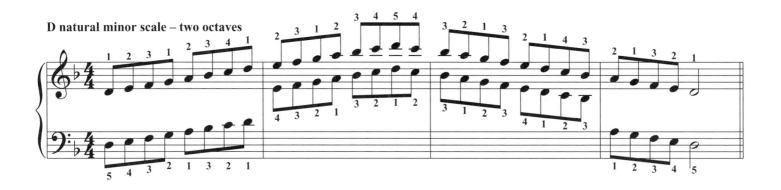

D harmonic minor scale – two octaves

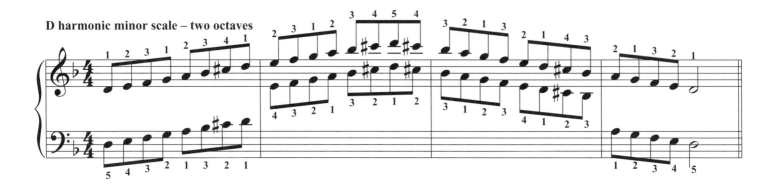

D harmonic minor scale – three octaves

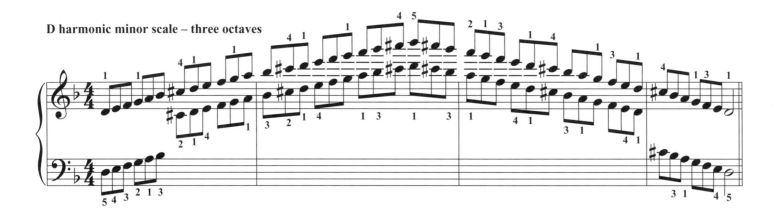

D harmonic minor scale – four octaves

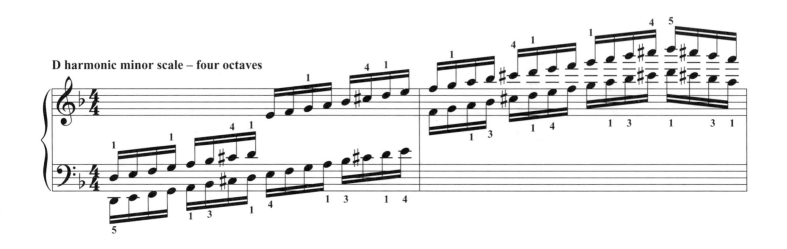

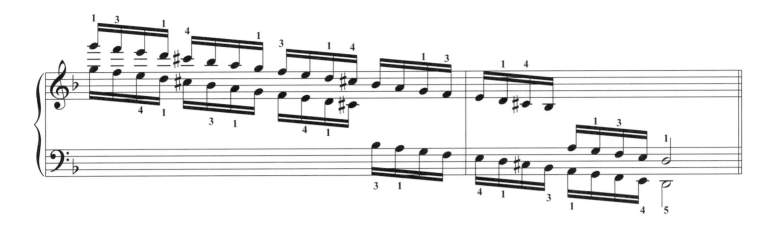

D melodic minor scale – two octaves

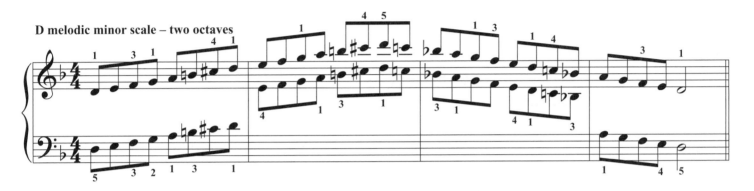

Chords of the D harmonic minor scale   **Primary chords – root position**

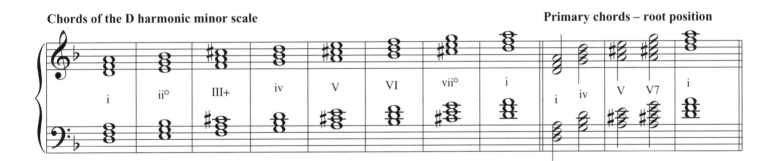

| i | ii° | III+ | iv | V | VI | vii° | i | | i | iv | V | V7 | i |

Blocked tonic inversions   **Broken tonic inversions**

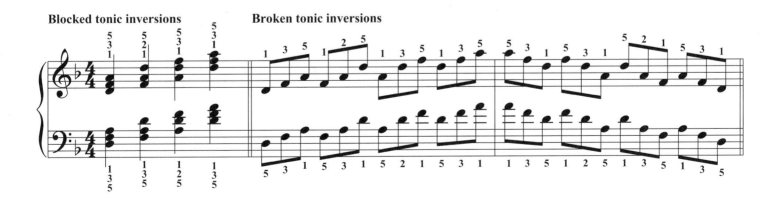

Cadences and inversions

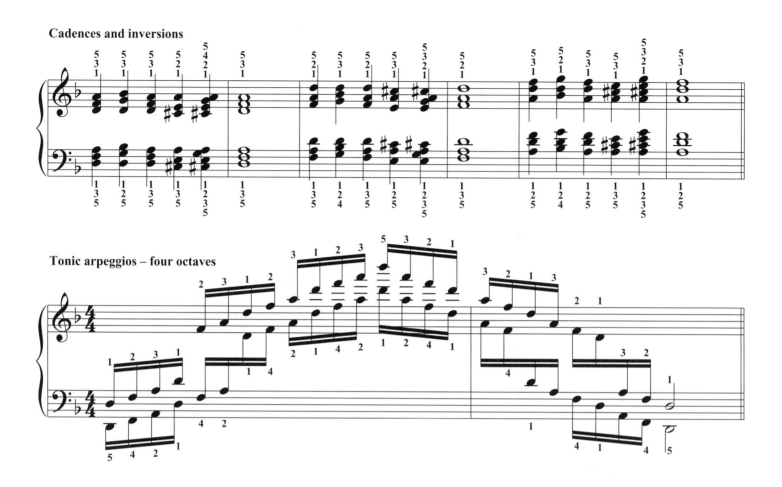

Tonic arpeggios – four octaves

C♯ diminished seventh arpeggios – two octaves, four positions

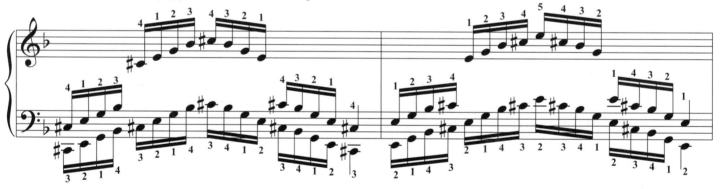

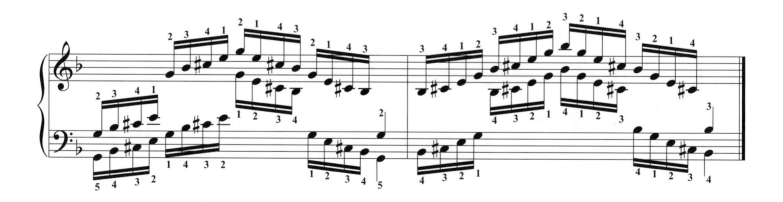

G natural minor scale – two octaves

G harmonic minor scale – two octaves

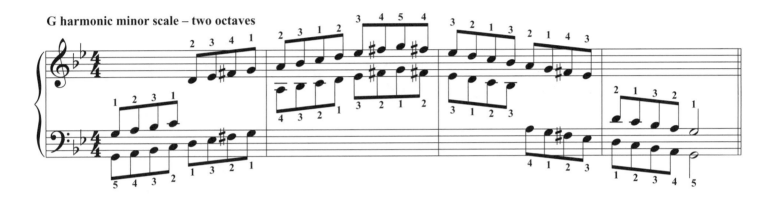

G harmonic minor scale – three octaves

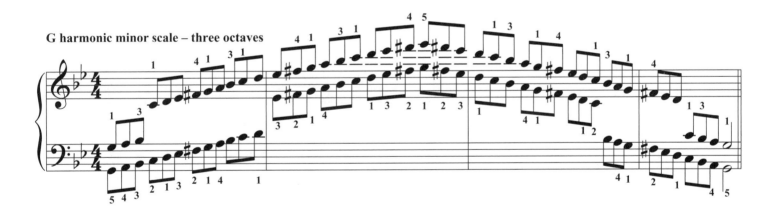

G harmonic minor scale – four octaves

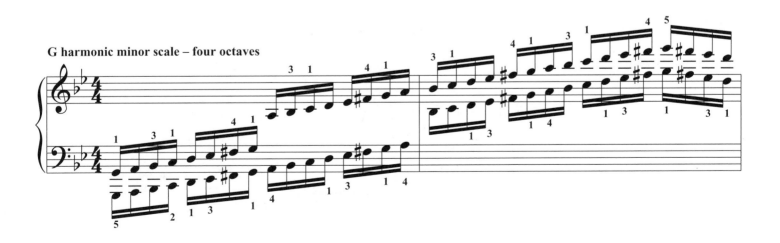

G melodic minor scale – two octaves

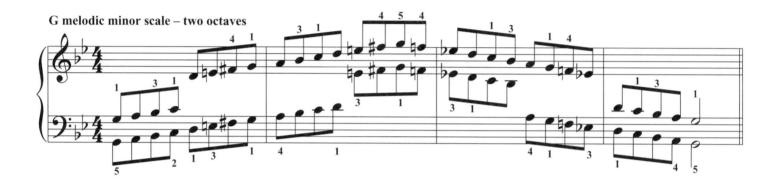

Chords of the G harmonic minor scale

Primary chords – root position

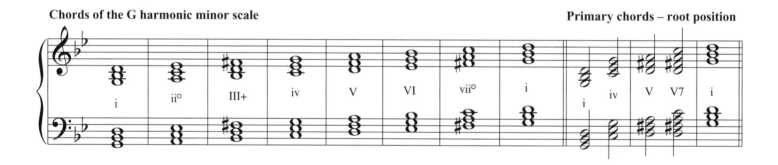

i   ii°   III+   iv   V   VI   vii°   i   i   iv   V   V7   i

Blocked tonic inversions

Broken tonic inversions

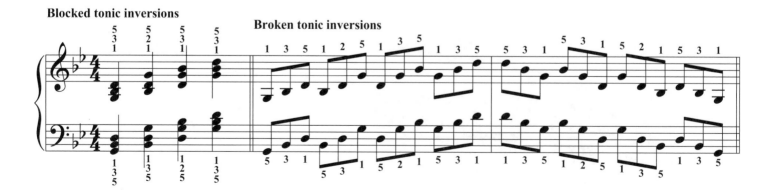

Cadences and inversions

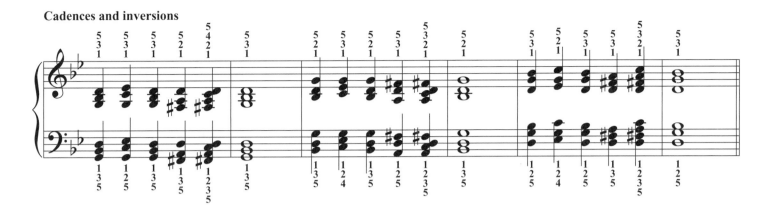

Tonic arpeggios – four octaves

F# diminished seventh arpeggios – two octaves, four positions

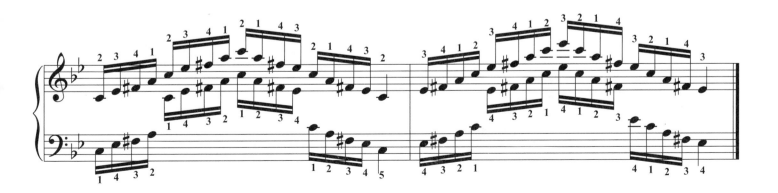

C natural minor scale – two octaves

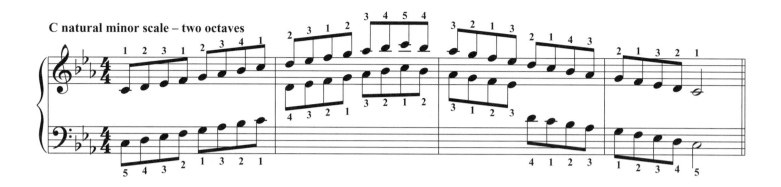

C harmonic minor scale – two octaves

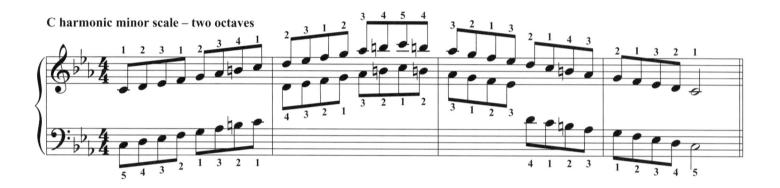

C harmonic minor scale – three octaves

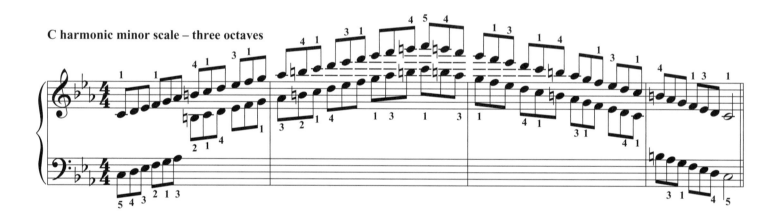

C harmonic minor scale – four octaves

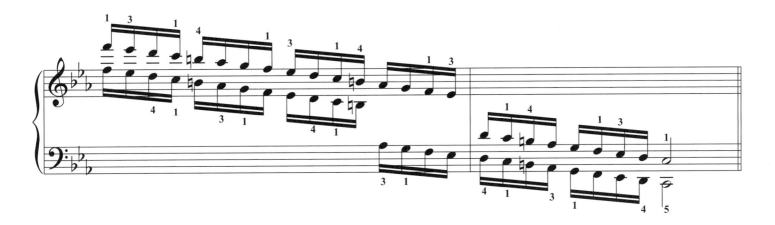

C melodic minor scale – two octaves

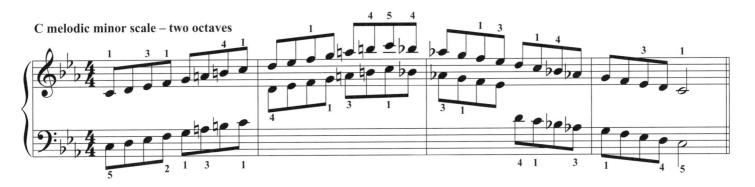

Chords of the C harmonic minor scale

Primary chords – root position

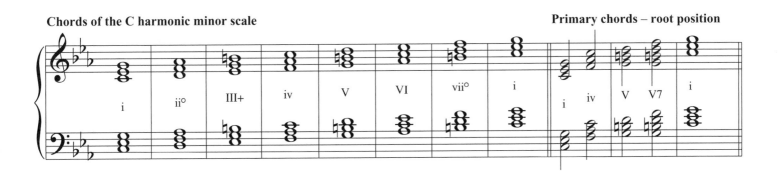

i   ii°   III+   iv   V   VI   vii°   i   i   iv   V   V7   i

Blocked tonic inversions

Broken tonic inversions

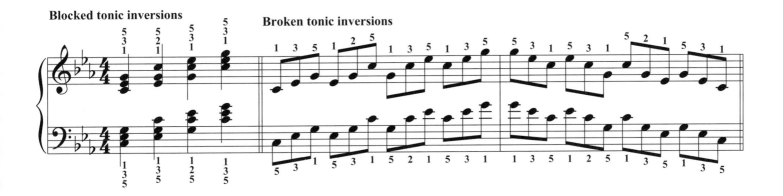

Cadences and inversions

Tonic arpeggios – four octaves

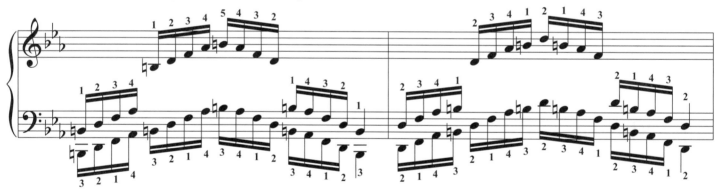

B diminished seventh arpeggios – two octaves, four positions

F natural minor scale – two octaves

F harmonic minor scale – two octaves

F harmonic minor scale – three octaves

F harmonic minor scale – four octaves

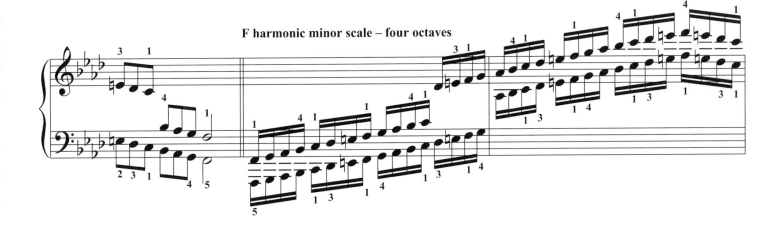

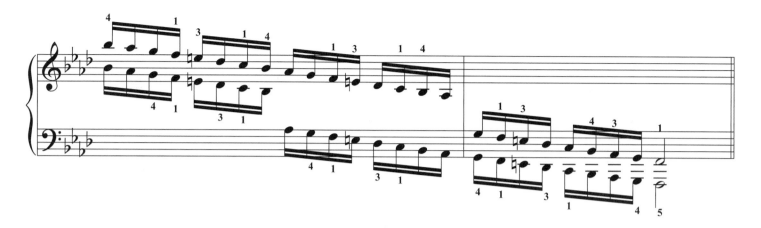

F melodic minor scale – two octaves

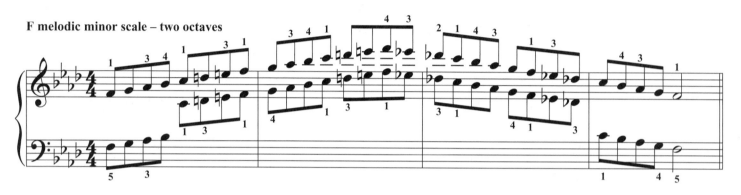

Chords of the F harmonic minor scale

Primary chords – root position

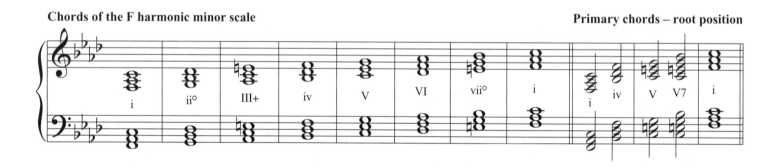

i ii° III+ iv V VI vii° i i iv V V7 i

Blocked tonic inversions

Broken tonic inversions

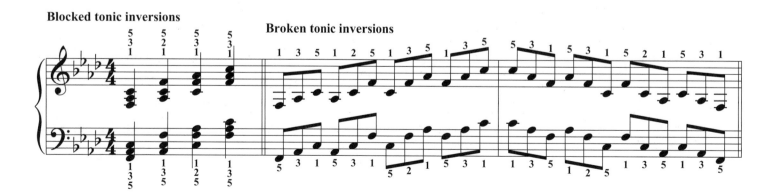

Cadences and inversions

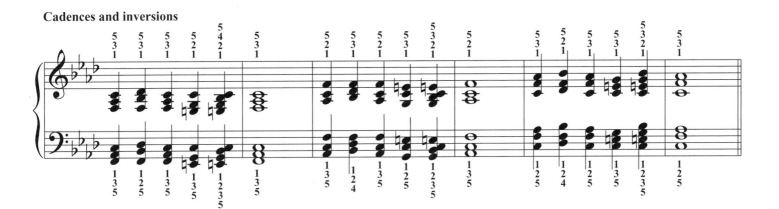

Tonic arpeggios – four octaves

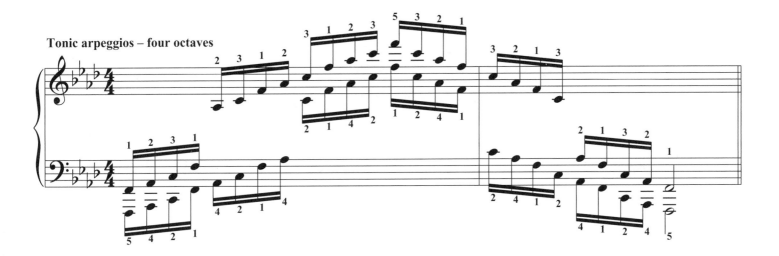

E diminished seventh arpeggios – two octaves, four positions

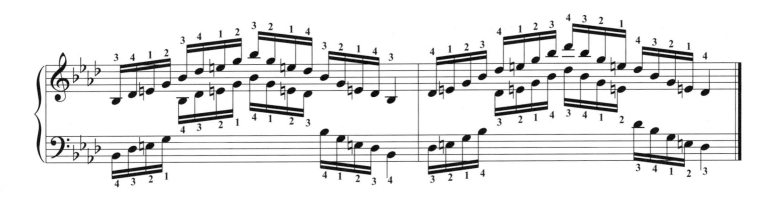

B♭ natural minor scale – two octaves

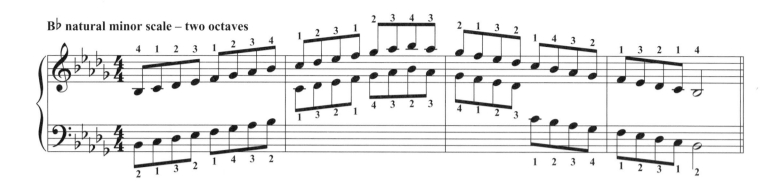

B♭ harmonic minor scale – two octaves

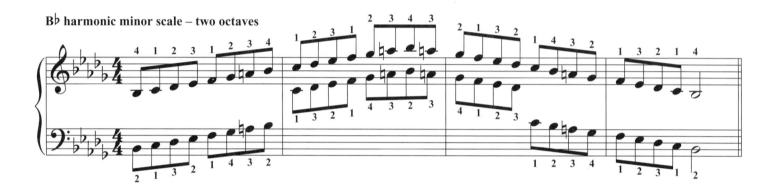

B♭ harmonic minor scale – three octaves

B♭ harmonic minor scale – four octaves

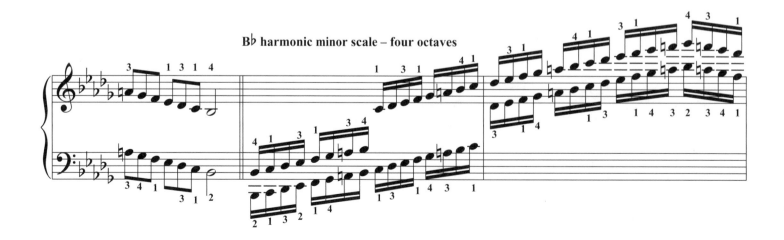

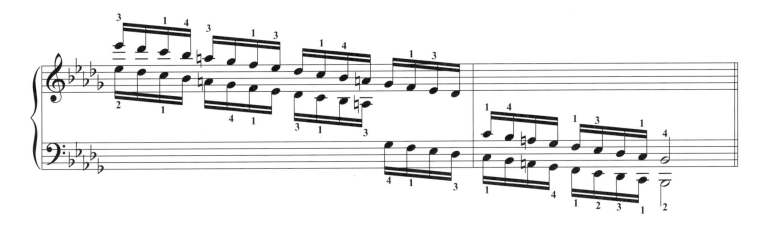

Bb melodic minor scale – two octaves

Chords of the Bb harmonic minor scale

Primary chords – root position

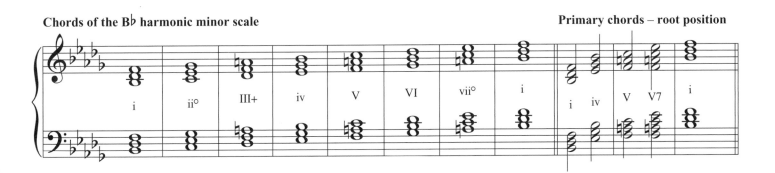

i   ii°   III+   iv   V   VI   vii°   i   i   iv   V   V7   i

Blocked tonic inversions

Broken tonic inversions

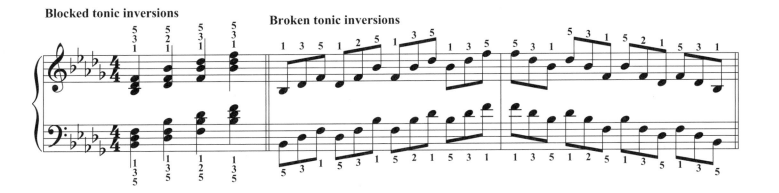

Cadences and inversions

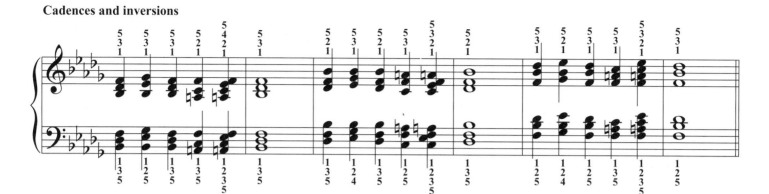

Tonic arpeggios – four octaves

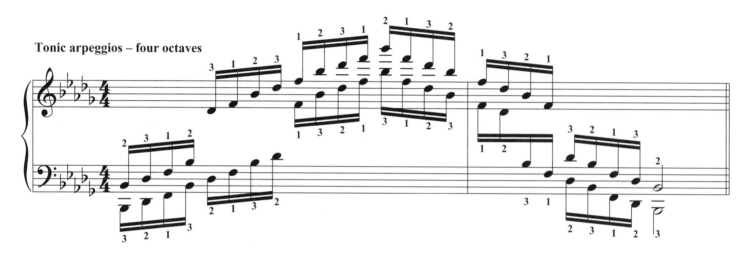

A diminished seventh arpeggios – two octaves, four positions

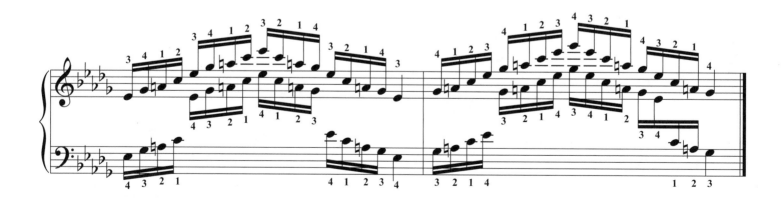

E♭ natural minor scale – two octaves

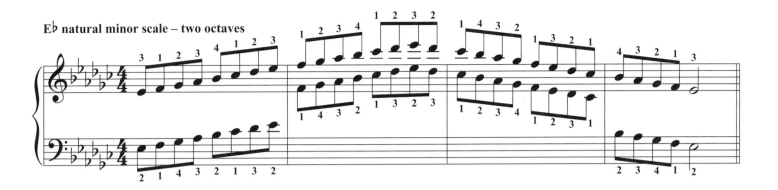

E♭ harmonic minor scale – two octaves

E♭ harmonic minor scale – three octaves

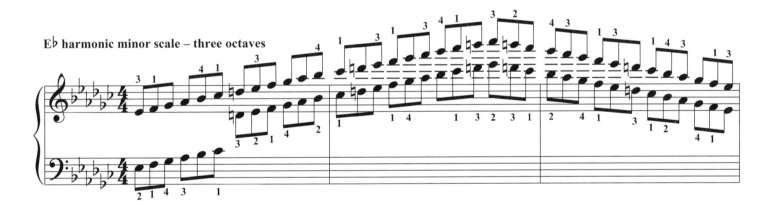

E♭ harmonic minor scale – four octaves

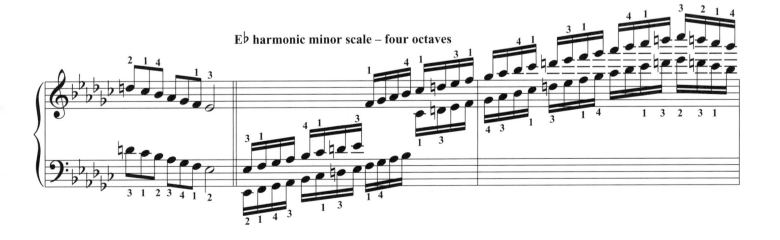

E♭ melodic minor scale – two octaves

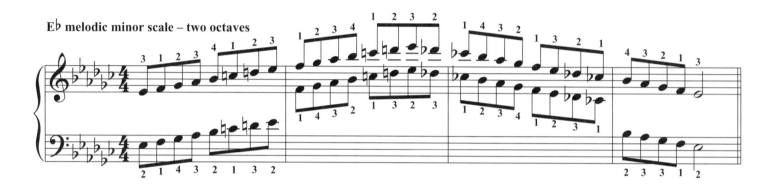

Chords of the E♭ harmonic minor scale   **Primary chords – root position**

i   ii°   III+   iv   V   VI   vii°   i   i   iv   V   V7   i

Blocked tonic inversions

Broken tonic inversions

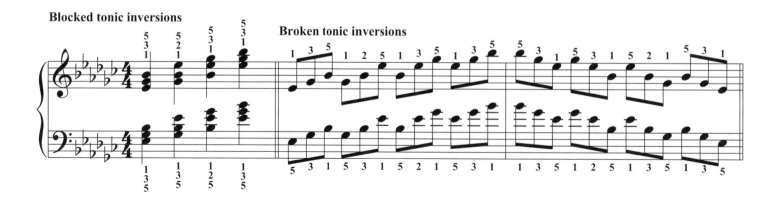

Cadences and inversions

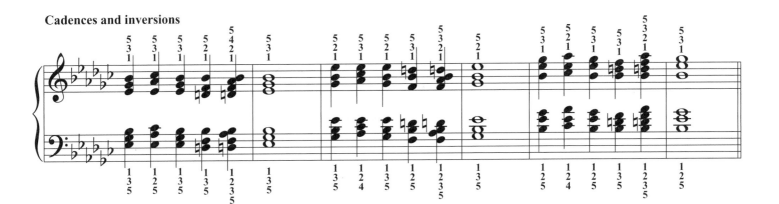

Tonic arpeggios – four octaves

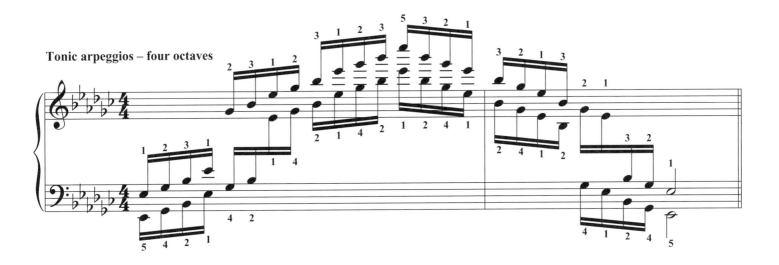

D diminished seventh arpeggios – two octaves, four positions

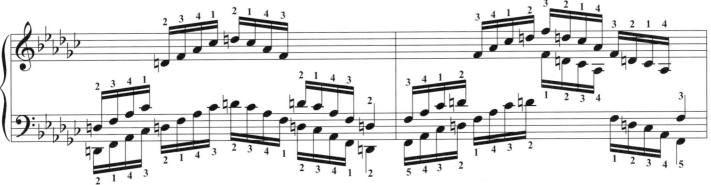

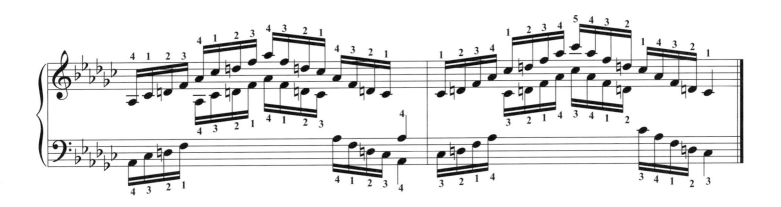

A♭ natural minor scale – two octaves

A♭ harmonic minor scale – two octaves

A♭ harmonic minor scale – three octaves

A♭ harmonic minor scale – four octaves

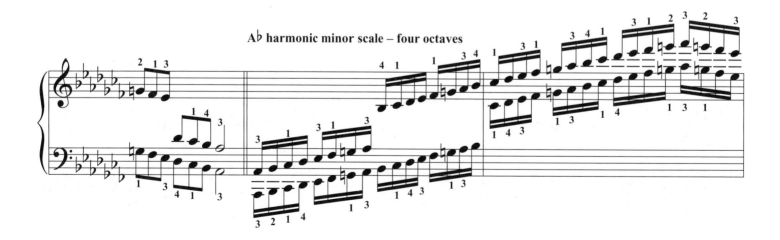

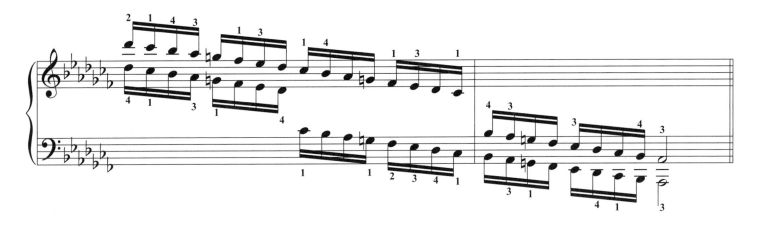

Ab melodic minor scale – two octaves

Chords of the Ab harmonic minor scale

Primary chords – root position

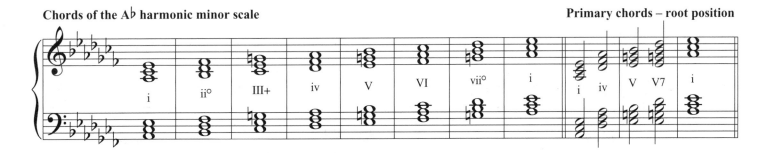

i   ii°   III+   iv   V   VI   vii°   i   i iv V V7 i

Blocked tonic inversions

Broken tonic inversions

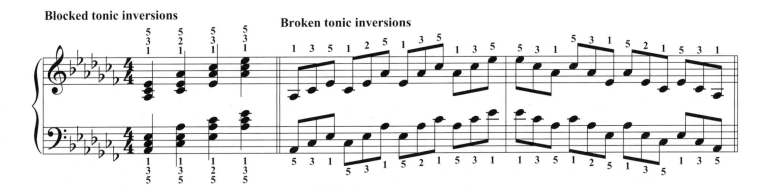

Cadences and inversions

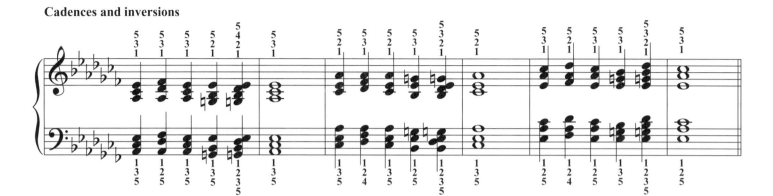

Tonic arpeggios – four octaves

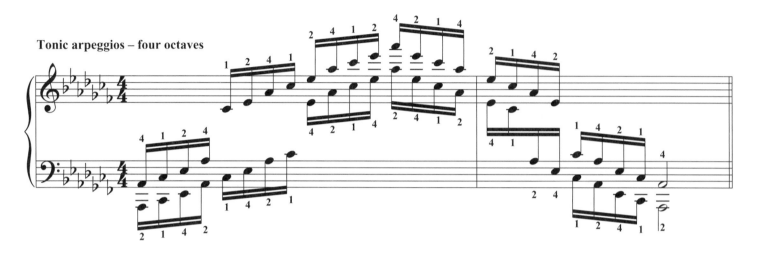

G diminished seventh arpeggios – two octaves, four positions

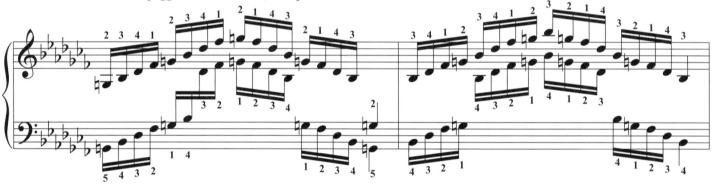

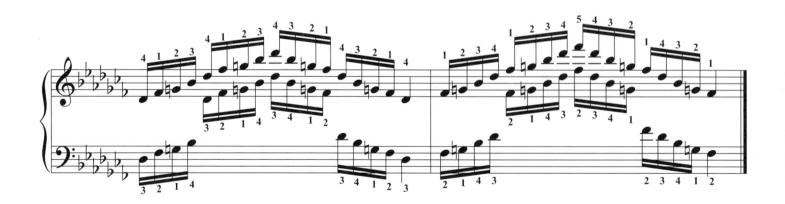

Practice suggestion: Start from various keys and play the chromatic scale hands separately and hands together. Use parallel and contrary motions.

Chromatic scale – parallel motion, two octaves

Chromatic scale – contrary motion, two octaves

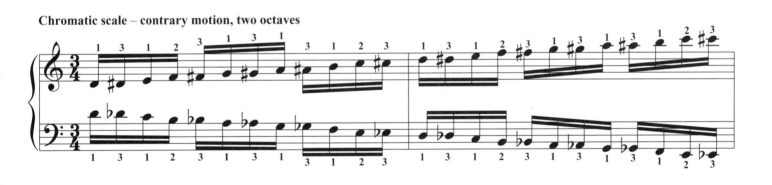

Practice suggestion: Transpose the scales in thirds and sixths to all major and minor keys.
Use the fingering as written with each major and minor scale in this book.

C major scale – thirds, two octaves

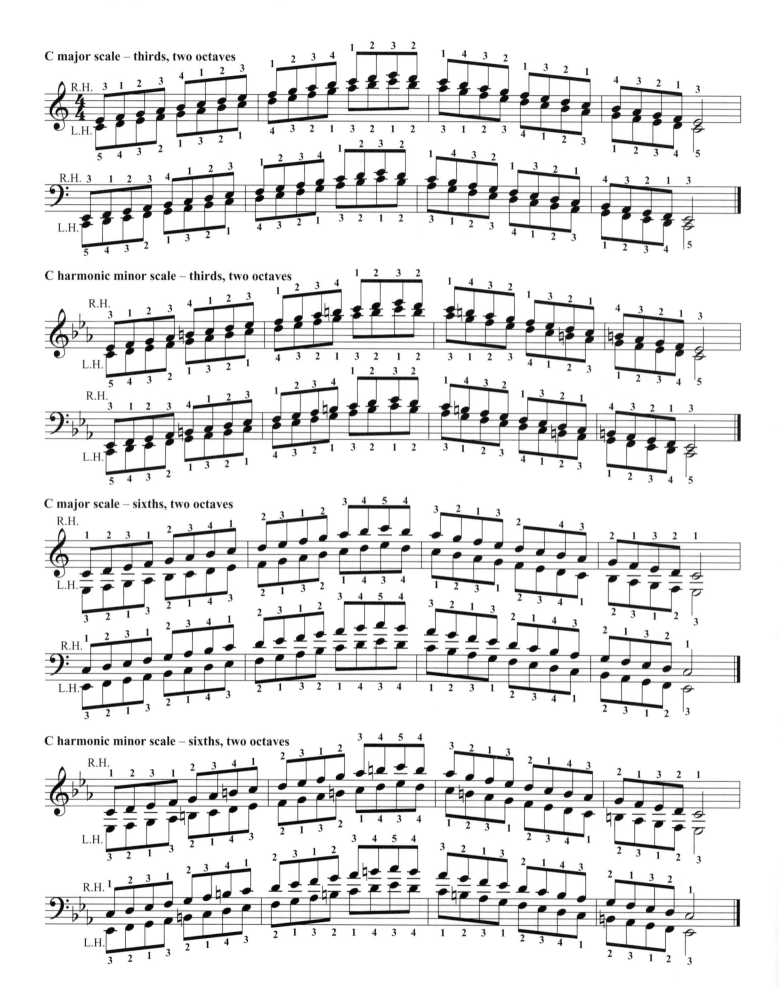

C harmonic minor scale – thirds, two octaves

C major scale – sixths, two octaves

C harmonic minor scale – sixths, two octaves

Practice suggestion: Use the Grand Scale form with all major and minor scales.

The Grand Scale in C Major

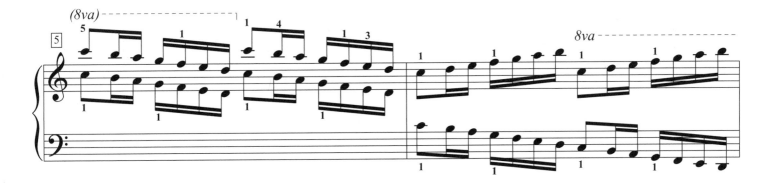

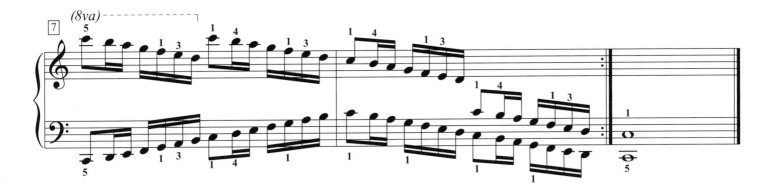

Chords Built on Each Scale Degree

Great Harmony & Theory Helpers

HAL LEONARD HARMONY & THEORY
by George Heussenstamm
Hal Leonard

These books are designed for anyone wishing to expand their knowledge of music theory, whether beginner or more advanced. The first two chapters deal with music fundamentals, and may be skipped by those with music reading experience.

00312062 Part 1 – Diatonic $27.50
00312064 Part 2 – Chromatic $27.50

BERKLEE MUSIC THEORY BOOK 1 – 2ND EDITION
by Paul Schmeling
Berklee Press

This essential method features rigorous, hands-on, "ears-on" practice exercises that help you explore the inner working of music, presenting notes, scales, and rhythms as they are heard in pop, jazz, and blues. You will learn and build upon the basic concepts of music theory with written exercises, listening examples, and ear training exercises.

50449615..$24.99

CONTEMPORARY COUNTERPOINT
Theory & Application
by Beth Denisch
Berklee Press

Use counterpoint to make your music more engaging and creative. Counterpoint – the relationship between musical voices – is among the core principles for writing music, and it has been central to the study of composition for many centuries. Whether you are a composer, arranger, film composer, orchestrator, music director, bandleader, or improvising musician, this book will help hone your craft, gain control, and lead you to new creative possibilities.

00147050..$22.99

THE CHORD WHEEL
The Ultimate Tool for All Musicians
by Jim Fleser
Hal Leonard

Master chord theory ... in minutes! *The Chord Wheel* is a revolutionary device that puts the most essential and practical applications of chord theory into your hands. This tool will help you: Improvise and Solo – Talk about chops! Comprehend key structure like never before; Transpose Keys – Instantly transpose any progression into each and every key; Compose Your Own Music – Watch your songwriting blossom! No music reading is necessary.

00695579..$15.99

ENCYCLOPEDIA OF READING RHYTHMS
Text and Workbook for All Instruments
by Gary Hess
Musicians Institute Press

A comprehensive guide to notes, rests, counting, subdividing, time signatures, triplets, ties, dotted notes and rests, cut time, compound time, swing, shuffle, rhythm studies, counting systems, road maps and more!

00695145..$29.99

HARMONY AND THEORY
A Comprehensive Source for All Musicians
by Keith Wyatt and Carl Schroeder
Musicians Institute Press

This book is a step-by-step guide to MI's well-known Harmony and Theory class. It includes complete lessons and analysis of: intervals, rhythms, scales, chords, key signatures; transposition, chord inversions, key centers; harmonizing the major and minor scales; and more!

00695161..$22.99

MUSIC THEORY WORKBOOK
For All Musicians
by Chris Bowman
Hal Leonard

A self-study course with illustrations and examples for you to write and check your answers. Topics include: major and minor scales; modes and other scales; harmony; intervals; chord structure; chord progressions and substitutions; and more.

00101379..$12.99

JAZZOLOGY
The Encyclopedia of Jazz Theory for All Musicians
by Robert Rawlins and Nor Eddine Bahha
Hal Leonard

A one-of-a-kind book encompassing a wide scope of jazz topics, for beginners and pros of any instrument. A three-pronged approach was envisioned with the creation of this comprehensive resource: as an encyclopedia for ready reference, as a thorough methodology for the student, and as a workbook for the classroom, complete with ample exercises and conceptual discussion.

00311167..$19.99

www.halleonard.com

PLAY PIANO LIKE A PRO!

AMAZING PHRASING – KEYBOARD
50 Ways to Improve Your Improvisational Skills
by Debbie Denke

Amazing Phrasing is for any keyboard player interested in learning how to improvise and how to improve their creative phrasing. This method is divided into three parts: melody, harmony, and rhythm & style. The online audio contains 44 full-band demos for listening, as well as many play-along examples so you can practice improvising over various musical styles and progressions.
00842030 Book/Online Audio... $16.99

BEBOP LICKS FOR PIANO
A Dictionary of Melodic Ideas for Improvisation
by Les Wise

Written for the musician who is interested in acquiring a firm foundation for playing jazz, this unique book/audio pack presents over 800 licks. By building up a vocabulary of these licks, players can connect them together in endless possibilities to form larger phrases and complete solos. The book includes piano notation, and the online audio contains helpful note-for-note demos of every lick.
00311854 Book/Online Audio... $17.99

BOOGIE WOOGIE FOR BEGINNERS
by Frank Paparelli

A short easy method for learning to play boogie woogie, designed for the beginner and average pianist. Includes: exercises for developing left-hand bass • 25 popular boogie woogie bass patterns • arrangements of "Down the Road a Piece" and "Answer to the Prayer" by well-known pianists • a glossary of musical terms for dynamics, tempo and style.
00120517 .... $10.99

HAL LEONARD JAZZ PIANO METHOD
by Mark Davis

This is a comprehensive and easy-to-use guide designed for anyone interested in playing jazz piano – from the complete novice just learning the basics to the more advanced player who wishes to enhance their keyboard vocabulary. The accompanying audio includes demonstrations of all the examples in the book! Topics include essential theory, chords and voicings, improvisation ideas, structure and forms, scales and modes, rhythm basics, interpreting a lead sheet, playing solos, and much more!
00131102 Book/Online Audio... $19.99

INTROS, ENDINGS & TURNAROUNDS FOR KEYBOARD
Essential Phrases for Swing, Latin, Jazz Waltz, and Blues Styles
by John Valerio

Learn the intros, endings and turnarounds that all of the pros know and use! This new keyboard instruction book by John Valerio covers swing styles, ballads, Latin tunes, jazz waltzes, blues, major and minor keys, vamps and pedal tones, and more.
00290525 .... $12.99

JAZZ PIANO TECHNIQUE
Exercises, Etudes & Ideas for Building Chops
by John Valerio

This one-of-a-kind book applies traditional technique exercises to specific jazz piano needs. Topics include: scales (major, minor, chromatic, pentatonic, etc.), arpeggios (triads, seventh chords, upper structures), finger independence exercises (static position, held notes, Hanon exercises), parallel interval scales and exercises (thirds, fourths, tritones, fifths, sixths, octaves), and more! The online audio includes 45 recorded examples.
00312059 Book/Online Audio... $19.99

JAZZ PIANO VOICINGS
An Essential Resource for Aspiring Jazz Musicians
by Rob Mullins

The jazz idiom can often appear mysterious and difficult for musicians who were trained to play other types of music. Long-time performer and educator Rob Mullins helps players enter the jazz world by providing voicings that will help the player develop skills in the jazz genre and start sounding professional right away – without years of study! Includes a "Numeric Voicing Chart," chord indexes in all 12 keys, info about what range of the instrument you can play chords in, and a beginning approach to bass lines.
00310914 .... $19.99

OSCAR PETERSON – JAZZ EXERCISES, MINUETS, ETUDES & PIECES FOR PIANO

Legendary jazz pianist Oscar Peterson has long been devoted to the education of piano students. In this book he offers dozens of pieces designed to empower the student, whether novice or classically trained, with the technique needed to become an accomplished jazz pianist.
00311225 .... $14.99

PIANO AEROBICS
by Wayne Hawkins

Piano Aerobics is a set of exercises that introduces students to many popular styles of music, including jazz, salsa, swing, rock, blues, new age, gospel, stride, and bossa nova. In addition, there is a online audio with accompaniment tracks featuring professional musicians playing in those styles.
00311863 Book/Online Audio $19.99

PIANO FITNESS
A Complete Workout
by Mark Harrison

This book will give you a thorough technical workout, while having fun at the same time! The accompanying online audio allows you to play along with a rhythm section as you practice your scales, arpeggios, and chords in all keys. Instead of avoiding technique exercises because they seem too tedious or difficult, you'll look forward to playing them. Various voicings and rhythmic settings, which are extremely useful in a variety of pop and jazz styles, are also introduced.
00311995 Book/Online Audio... $19.99

HAL•LEONARD®
7777 W. BLUEMOUND RD. P.O. BOX 13819
MILWAUKEE, WISCONSIN 53213
www.halleonard.com